Hoof It! 7 Key Lessons on your journey of success

Dedication

I dedicate this book to...

My father, who I miss beyond measure, who inspired me to always give of my best, who taught me the true meaning of integrity, and who left a legacy for me to pass on to my children;

My wife, Nancy, who I love increasingly with each day, who I have been blessed to share my life with, and who has always believed in me;

My children, Dreanna and Jensen, who are a constant source of joy to me, who teach me so much about what love and purpose are all about, and who are my legacy to the world;

And to my Lord, who is my strength and without whom I would not be able to deliver this message.

7 Key Lessons on your Journey of Success

Dr Richard Norris

Hoof it!
First published in 2010 by;
Ecademy Press
48 St Vincent Drive, St Albans, Herts, AL1 5SJ
info@ecademy-press.com
www.ecademy-press.com

Printed and Bound by; Lightning Source in the UK and USA
Book interior Karen Gladwell
Cover artwork and design by Michael Inns

Printed on acid-free paper from managed forests. This book is
printed on demand, so no copies will be remaindered or pulped.

ISBN 978-1-905823-83-3

Contents

Dr Richard Norris MBA

Richard's purpose is to bring transformation to people's lives so that they are living to fulfil their purpose whether at work, rest or play.

From a veterinarian delivering calves and doing eyelid surgery on leopards to an army officer responsible for security and animal welfare to a post-grad student in internal medicine and an MBA to unemployed to an award-winning business coach and business development strategist, Richard's own success journey has been dynamic and diverse. Along the way he has also captained, coached and motivated sports individuals and teams to realize their potential.

What became apparent is that Richard truly excels at challenging the status quo and clients to be better, to do better and to attain better results across their lives, businesses and organizations. That applies whether working with entrepreneurs or executives, leaders or followers, individuals or teams.

Richard contributes articles to various publications on-line and in print on a range of topics around business, leadership and personal success. He also presents, speaks, and lectures across various institutions, conferences and events around the globe.

As a competitive swimmer for 23 years, Richard lives by the adage a healthy body is a healthy mind. Today Richard continues to get his endorphin fix whether in the gym, on the road or in a pool. Richard is a lifelong learner and has invested significantly in his own personal development. He understands the power of applied learning that allows for growth and delivers results simply, effectively and consistently. With an absolute belief that inside everyone is greatness, Richard, by example and passion, uniquely inspires this belief in others.

Introduction

This writing of this book has been inspired by my years of coaching individuals, teams and businesses. It breathes the life lessons my own father instilled within me as I grew up. It relates my observations of success in business, sport and life. As such, this book has been written to enable you to progress your success, and ensures the same of every other person who picks it up, reads it and applies the lessons taught within.

It is worth emphasizing that success is a relative term; what success means to you is likely to be different to what it means to me or to any other person. Know for sure, however, that you have a purpose here on Earth. Discover it. Live it. And when you do, you will know what success truly means for you — and how to achieve it.

When you are able to identify your purpose, this book will help to catalyze your success, both now and in the future. It is noteworthy to highlight that this book is not intended to be read only once; it is instead intended to be a constant reference for those times in your life when you need to know what are the next best steps, or even just to seek a bit of guidance from the many pages of both musings and evidence.

"How?" you ask. Well, this book has been created and written around seven key lessons pertaining to your Journey of Success, with each lesson being reinforced from chapter to chapter.

For each key lesson, there is an exercise at the end of the respective chapter. These exercises are designed to give you focus on those key insights and actions pertaining to the lesson concerned.

My intention is that by the end of this book you will have an action plan which will enable you to progress towards your success based on your current circumstances, and to ultimately achieve the goals outlined within that plan. As you accomplish your aims and achieve your success, refer back to the book again and to each of the lessons. Discover new insights. Create a new plan. Continue your Journey. And then do it all again.

Now all that remains is for you to begin to . . . *Hoof it!*

Richard Norris- *June 2010*

For more information about Richard Norris's workshops, webinars, speaking engagements, coaching programs and other resources, please visit

www.hoofitbook.com

Prologue

February. The sun is already shimmering above the horizon as it begins its arc across the early morning azure blue sky. The wind is timid at best; barely stirring the tall verdant swathes of grass, and now carries with it the soft hint of cool, refreshing, life-giving rain. In the distance, a slow, building rumble of thunder can be heard, confirming the promise carried on the wind. Far aloft already, the vultures coast the skies, riding in ominous circles where the thermals rise from the heated plains.

The Serengeti is already vibrantly alive, and the vast, seemingly-mixed Herds of wildlife slowly mill across the grasslands. The Journey is about to begin again or, rather, to continue.

This year, there seems to be even more animals on the plains than in previous years, each competing for their life essentials: food, water and space. Life must go on. And so it does — it's calving season.

Amongst the milling, snorting Wildebeest Herd, beneath the meager shade of an acacia tree, a new life is about to be born. The birth represents only one special life of the 500,000 expected to be added to the Herd this year. And it is here that this story begins.

Within this group of cows, one was having a particularly difficult time; Moh had been laboring for the past hour. Time was pressing, and she was beginning to worry. Even though she had purposefully placed herself within the center of the dispersed Herd, if the calf didn't arrive soon, her nursery Herd would move on. She was the last cow due to give birth.

The rule is to keep moving forward and not to unnecessarily expose yourself. At such a time as this, Lion and Hyena were always nearby, always a threat, always looking to spy the weakest and most vulnerable. Already, there was the distaste of unease for the nearby cows, as they gently but watchfully encouraged their newborn calves to suckle and test out their gangly legs.

Moh let out a series of heavy, broken groans.

And then finally, after one final contraction, there, lying glistening amongst the blades of grass, struggled that which appeared to be nothing more than a jumble of mismatched legs.

Moh staggered to her feet and looked wondrously down upon this new bundle of joy; she was overwhelmed by the power of her love for this — her first calf.

"How wonderful! It's a boy!" she exclaimed to everyone and yet no one in particular.

"Isn't he beautiful? I think I'll call him Vic... Yes! Vic it is!"

In response, there was a little snort at her feet. A small pink tongue peaked out through black lips and curled upwards to lick its muzzle. Moh nudged her calf and began to lick its face clean with her coarse tongue, meanwhile breathing in deeply to imprint the smell of her son. A gentle mewling sound greeted her efforts, and Vic began to breathe more deeply.

"Hurry up, Moh! The Herd is getting restless," Bet urged.

Since joining the Circle of Life, Bet and Moh had grown up through the Herd together. Bet had her female calf a few days ago; little Ama now tentatively nuzzled Vic too.

"Hey, Vic, you want to play?" little Ama asked innocently.

Vic responded with seemingly spasmodic movements and then began to rock and sway as he pulled himself to his feet.

"If we don't get moving soon, we'll be left behind," Bet declared with a trace of fear in her words.

Now was a critical time. Within no more than a few minutes, Vic needed to be up, needed to suckle and needed to be able to run. And then, almost as if on–cue, Vic managed to untangle his legs, get his slender and gawky back legs out from under him, and pushed up enough to gain balance on his knees. Moh gently put her muzzle under his chest and lifted, being careful not to hurt him with her curving horns. Vic's legs seemed to come to life and, within seconds, he was standing, and it is of no concern that his legs were a bit splayed and, yes, well, wobbly.

Moh quickly directed Vic to her udder to suckle; all mothers knew the first meal was always the most important. With each swallow, Vic visibly appeared to become stronger and straighter on his legs. Indeed, Vic now looked like a typical Wildebeest calf – a mirror of an adult – with his gray coat, the rudiments of a black mane, and a typical lop-sidedness with a comparatively heavy fore body and those slender haunches.

"Moh, we really must go. Soon, we'll become stragglers and we don't want that," Bet urged.

"Give me a minute to help Vic," replied Moh, and then directed her attention to her son.

"Vic, do you feel strong enough to walk and keep up with your momma?"

"Yes, Momma," Vic uttered hesitantly, surprised by the sound of his own voice.

"Good. Let's go."

And with that, Moh began to move away and, as if still joined by that umbilical cord, Vic moved awkwardly after his mother to join the moving Herd. Soon, they were seemingly lost in the moving throng.

Chapter One

A few days later, across the plains, there was tension in the air — a mixture of both positive and negative energy. Predator and prey alike sensed that the Journey was about to begin for yet another year, and with it came a spectrum of thoughts and emotions never absent whenever embarking on something new or renewed. For some, there was the eager anticipation for the start of another migration — for the hope, belief and the promise it would bring of abundance; for others, it was a mixture of both excitement and trepidation as they faced something so big that they could not quite comprehend it and could only fathom it from the stories of those who have gone before. Finally, for others it was something that only held a great fear: Fear of the unknown; fear of what may or may not happen along the way.

In short, life here on the Serengeti mirrored what existed everywhere, what existed amongst every living creature. There were two general threads of thinking: The first focused on going forward; the other on looking backwards.

Regardless, what they expected will happen, will generally happen. It was the Way of Things.

Suddenly, amidst an unusually still moment where all life seemed to be holding its breath, a deep resonant bellow erupted from the center of the Herd.

"MMMUUUUOOOOOUUUUNNNNHHH!!!!"

It was time! This was the signal all had been waiting for. The Journey had begun.

For today, with his mother nearby, Vic had been grazing with no apparent purpose, alongside Ama with whom Vic had become good friends. In fact, they had become already inseparable.

As the bellow reached Vic's ears, he could feel an uneasiness stirring within him. "Momma!! What was that? What does it mean? Who made that sound?" Vic asked in quick succession.

With a smile Moh answered, "That was what we have all been waiting for. The Call. Now that all the calves have been born, the Call tells us and the rest of the animals of the plains that it is time to move. It is time to begin the Journey in search of new sources of grass and water."

"But, Momma, I like it here!" exclaimed Vic.

"Vic, that may be true, but if we do not move we will run out of food and water. We will return many suns in the future as the Journey always brings us back here."

"But if it brings us back here then why can't we stay?" asked Vic with his still apparent child-like logic.

Moh looked bemused, as she had had a constant barrage of questions ever since Vic took his first breath. "Life is about moving on and not staying still. It is the Way of Things," Moh replied with great patience.

And just then, like a ripple on a lake, the Herd began to move — or at least this part of it did; it took time for the reaction of the Call to reach the center of the Herd where all the cows and their calves were protected.

> *Life is about moving on and not staying still.*
> *It is the Way of Things.*

The protection the calves and their mothers have shared up until now was no more; with the Herd beginning to move, the Wildebeest would now be arrayed in groups, columns, strays and stragglers. At such a time as this, the perils of the Journey moved from the realms of stories to an almost tangible presence, which probed the limits the Herd.

During previous days, Moh and Bet had heard that some Lion had attacked the edges of the Herd. As the Herd slowly moved on, there was the realization that the problem had been one that only others had been forced to face. Now, however, would be different; they had calves to look after and the Journey ahead of them — and both of them felt a certain ominous concern for what lay ahead.

With that, and almost in perfect unison, both Moh and Bet called out as they too started to move in the general direction of everyone else, "Children, come here. Keep close."

Once Vic and Ama had trotted over, Moh added, "Keep up please. There will be times when we will need to run, so when you see us begin to run, don't ask questions, just run and stay at our sides".

At once, both Vic and Ama looked at each other and then at their mothers, before nodding their heads and acknowledging in chorus, "Yes, Momma!"

And with that, all four of them began to walk after the Wildebeest in front of them.

For Vic, the view was anything but exciting. Being a calf, he could only see so much around him. With the memory of running in the open grasslands and grazing at his leisure, Vic decided it was not much fun staring only at the hindquarters of adults all around him. Now his nostrils were filling with dust and his eyes were blinking out the grit. He looked over at Ama who was ambling alongside; she ambled with her head down, looking similarly unimpressed.

"Ama?" Vic enquired hoping to get her attention.

No response.

"Ama!" Vic snorted loudly.

That startled Ama. She shook off her walking trance. "Huh... What?"

"I'm bored. You fancy an adventure?"

"What do you call this? We're on the Journey."

"I know that. I mean, well, when we stop for the night, do you fancy heading to the limits of the Herd? We never actually get to see anything here. I want to explore a bit and see the Edge. I want to know what's out there. Who knows what's beyond the Herd. I want to see it with my own eyes and not just hear about it."

"You know what our moms would say."

"Yes, but if we're not around to hear them say it, then it doesn't really matter, does it?"

Ama couldn't disagree with such logic, especially when it was genius enough to allow them to break free from their boundaries. So, with that, the two of them looked at each other and smiled knowingly. This would be fun.

The Journey always began with heading towards the setting sun. The first moon phase of the Journey always coincided with breeding season, which added further danger for the calves with frustration and aggression oozing from the bulls. Separations between the cow and calf did often occur; usually these separations were short-lived. Occasionally, however, they could easily become permanent.

Dusk gently descended and with it the pace of day-life slowed and night-life built up. It was a time of transition. Day to night. Light to dark. For the Herd, it meant moving forward to rest. For Vic and Ama, it meant restlessness and excitement. For the dominant bulls it was an ideal time to stake some territory and win the affections of the cows.

The nursery group in which Moh and Vic were traveling began to seek shelter in the lee of a cluster of acacia trees near a watering hole. The cows trusted their maternal instincts and decided it is a good place to rest.

Watchfully, one by one, the cows and their calves began to settle down for much needed rest. They remained watchful for the bulls and for any signs of Lion or Hyena stalking; although this was a time for rest, it was also a time for heightened awareness.

As always, the cows aligned themselves with their calves, all facing the same direction to ensure that, when necessary, they could move quickly, maintain orientation and move as one. They knew, like all creatures moving in packs or Herds, there was safety in numbers, and it was paramount not to become one of the stragglers.

Just as Moh had picked a spot next to a lone, rounded boulder that seemed to be propping up the tree next to it, Vic asked, "Mom, can I go see Ama?"

"What for, Vic? We have been traveling all day and we need some rest."

Vic finished on a flattering note, hoping it would sway his mother. "Well, Ama and I have decided that at the end of each day we'd like to share with each other what we have learned and what went well for us. That way we can grow smart like you, Mom!"

"Hmm," Moh murmured hesitantly. "Well... okay then, but—"

"Great!" exclaimed Vic, interrupting his mother and, with that, began to head off.

"Vic, not so fast!" Moh interjected. "You can go on two conditions,"

Turning to look, Vic uttered with resignation, "Sure, Mom. What are they?"

Vic could hardly hide his excitement at being off to the Edge; the Edge was the outer limits of the Herd and where the real threat of danger and attack was most real. Vic knew the dangers, but it was also the ultimate place to experience first hand all that was new.

Vic and Ama had agreed, they would head further into the middle of the group so as to allay any concerns their mothers may have. From there, they would break off toward the Edge.

"First, give me a nuzzle goodbye," Moh stipulated.

"Ahh, Mom!"

With a direct stare at Vic, Moh added, "And second, you must promise me that you'll go directly to Bet and Ama and be back before it gets completely dark."

"Sure, Mom," Vic hastily replied.

With a quick trot over to give his mother a nuzzle, Vic quickly turned and trotted away and around the other side of the boulder towards where Bet and Ama have settled for the evening. Soon enough, Vic saw Ama heading towards him.

So far, so good. Their plan was working.

Meeting up with Ama under the biggest acacia tree, Vic excitedly burst out, "It worked! Now we can head to the Edge!"

With a cautioning whisper, Ama urged, "Be quiet! Do you want everyone to know what we are up to?"

"No, no, of course not. I am just so excited!" Vic exclaimed.

Just then, a large bull loomed ominously, heading in the direction from which Vic had come. With his magnificent curving horns, a thick, coarse mane, shiny black hooves and huge shoulders, he was the most incredible bull Vic had ever seen in his young life. Vic froze in awe at the figure which was now towering over them.

Disdainfully, the bull queried, "What are you two doing here? Shouldn't you both be with your mothers?"

"Ye… Ye… Yes, Sir. We are just heading to them now," stuttered Vic respectfully.

"Good. Carry on." And with that the bull continued past them with barely a glance. Vic and Ama looked at each other with relief. Now they could get back to moving to the Edge.

"Let's go," whispered Vic excitedly.

Quietly and carefully, the two young calves turned and set off toward the Edge. As they picked their way through the numerous prone forms, Vic and Ama realized the group was actually much bigger than they initially thought; they had only ever been near the center of the nursery group and so had not realized it would take so long to tip-hoof their way through.

Ama began to get uneasy. "Vic, I think we should go back. It's close to being dark already, and we are not even at the Edge yet."

"Don't be silly, Ama! We've come this far. I want to see what's out there."

"Vic, I want to go back," Ama replied tremulously.

"Why? Are you afraid?!"

"Yes, I am," confessed Ama as she came to a halt.

"What are you stopping for?" Vic asked irritably.

"I told you, I want to go back. It's not what I was expecting."

"What you expect and what you get can be different things. If you want to head back to your mom, then go — I'm not stopping you. But I'm going ahead."

"Vic, you mustn't. Please come back with me," pleaded Ama.

"No!" Vic replied defiantly, "I'm going to the Edge — with or without you!"

"Please, Vic!"

"No!"

Vic then turned and headed off on a tangent toward the Edge. Ama stayed rooted to the ground until she realized that Vic was not coming back. Reluctantly, she too turned but headed back towards her mother and comparative safety.

Meanwhile, Vic kept his eyes firmly fixed ahead of him, his thoughts building on the wonder of what he would find. Already, he could picture himself on the Edge, looking out onto the vast expanse of plains, wondering what further adventures lay ahead, what wondrous creatures and beauty would be beyond his gaze, all waiting to be explored.

Lost in reverie, Vic hadn't noticed that there were fewer and fewer Wildebeest around. And then, like a slap to his senses, he realized that the night air was now full of new sounds and new smells. He stopped. With a dawning awareness, both Vic's heart and mind accelerated as he realized he had crossed the Edge.

"WOW!" Vic exclaimed to no one in particular. After all, no one was around anyway.

Vic looked up and could see the sky speckled with the radiant glory of a myriad of twinkling stars. Their flickering light was enthralling. The cicadas were in full chorus. The breeze here was fresh as it lazily caressed his nostrils. Mesmerized by what he was witnessing, an alarm bell then slowly began ringing towards a crescendo in Vic's head.

And then, as he pulled himself from the starry trance, Vic's eyes noticed two things — and his nose acknowledged another. Firstly, he realized there was no moonlight and, secondly, his peripheral vision just barely detected some dark shapes moving towards him, low to the ground and almost imperceptibly. A strong pungent odor caused his nostrils to twitch.

Not having ever seen a predator, but having heard various stories from the elders of the Herd — which he had thought at the time had been told and fabricated just to scare him and the other calves of the nursery — Vic suddenly felt unease stir in his stomachs and the taste of panic flood into his mouth. And, for the first moment since his and Ama's departure, he questioned his decision as he felt in his guts that he was dangerously close to some prowling predators. Or rather, they were very near to him.

Backing up slowly with trembling legs, Vic kept his eyes, muzzle and ears straining ahead of him. Now he knew what it meant to be afraid.

"Ama had been right. I should have turned back," thought Vic, full of fear.

Vic was snapped out of his thoughts as his ears detected a growing rhythmic soft rustling along with the sound of breathing speeding closer. His brain registered that several forms were heading toward him — forms which had been described to him as that of a Lion.

With that realization, Vic lost all sense of reason. He turned and fled as fast as his hooves could find ground underneath them bellowing, "LION! LION! LION!"

Fortunately, Vic had been close enough to the Herd that he was almost upon it as he began to flee. In a mad panic, he kept running, dodging bewildered, alarmed and, now stampeding, Wildebeest.

Vic began to cry, "Momma! Momma! Momma!" in between gasps as he ran for his life with no real direction other than to stick close to any other animal that looked like it, too, was fleeing.

For what seemed hours, Vic continued to run and call out for his mother. He came across a variety of other animals which had joined the swelling stampede: Impala, Gazelle, Eland and Zebra. Vic panicked more and more as he saw less and less Wildebeest. His throat quickly became hoarse from crying out.

After some time, Vic almost imperceptibly realized that the other animals around him had slowed, albeit warily. Vic would have kept running but he was both exhausted and scared. He quickly realized that there is safety in numbers and it would be better if he was not exposed.

Some time had passed. It was still dark and there were still several hours yet until morning. Wondering where the Herd was and, more importantly, where his mother was, Vic looked around desperately. Noticing a large group of Zebra settling down, Vic stumbled toward them. Upon approaching them, he cleared his dry throat as best he could and asked,

"Can I j... j... join you, please? I got lost in the stampede and cannot find my Herd."

One Zebra nodded to the ground beside her, "Of course. Rest here, little one".

With no need for encouragement, Vic dropped to the ground and fell immediately to sleep with a pervasive thought in his mind: I'm alone.

Vic woke with a start. His heart was in his throat fighting the fear of the nightmare which had been plaguing his sleep. He had been being chased by a black shadow that was closing in on him, separating him from the Herd and filling him with dread. With the bitter aftertaste of the nightmare still lingering tenaciously on his conscious thoughts, Vic began to calm down slightly — but only slightly; after all, in part, the nightmare was now a reality. He was, like in his dreams, alone, and was desperate to find his mother and the rest of his Herd. But where would he start?

Still huddled amongst the Zebras, Vic began to take stock of what his senses were telling him. The first rays of light were creeping over the horizon in the east, casting the day's first tendrils of light and warmth across the landscape. The air was still but was tattooed with the distant mimicking cries of buzzards aloft, patrolling for signs of a meal.

With the thought of food, Vic's stomachs came to life instantaneously with a churning grumble. He was hungry. Very hungry. What he wouldn't give for some of his mother's warm, comforting milk.

Thinking about food wasn't helping. Vic had to do something about it. A dilemma began to surface in Vic's head, and the next thing he knew, he was speaking to himself.

"I need to find my Momma but I also need to find food and, come to think of it, something to drink. What should I do?"

Next to him, the female Zebra who had invited Vic to join their group was just stirring and directed her gaze toward him, interrupting his monologue.

"Dear, I think you would be wise to eat first and get your strength up if you want to find your mother. You can join us," she offered. "We are heading in generally the same direction as the Wildebeest. At least you will be somewhat safer than if you were going alone."

"Thank you," mombled Vic.

Meanwhile, all around Vic the other Zebra and their foals were getting to their feet and stretching their legs and necks in an odd combination of ways, working out the kinks from their restoring sleep. The foals were looking for their first feed of the day and the conversation amongst the adults was centered around the stampede the night before and where the nearest watering hole might be.

Vic was only loosely paying attention to all that was going on around him; while he would have no doubt benefited from observing and learning something about other Herds, he was nevertheless preoccupied with when he could get back to his mother. Interestingly, he noted that he unquestionably intended to get back to her; there was no question of if — 'if' gives the option of considering failure or maybe not even trying, but 'when' makes the aim more purposeful, and makes the possibility of success seem that much more likely.

Just then, Vic noticed that the conversation had turned to action. The Zebra were moving West, albeit slowly. And, despite the group being of sufficient size to hide him and despite his being invited to join them, Vic still felt exposed and alone. As best he could, he stuck as close as he could to the young mare he had slept next to; he wanted to hide in the midst of the Herd, to feel more protected. But, that area of protection was for the foals.

Vic concluded that now he had experienced more than his fill of the Edge.

'If' gives the option of considering failure or at least not trying. 'When' makes the aim more purposeful.

"Why oh why didn't I just stay put and not seek out adventure? I should have stayed with Momma. Or I should have turned back with Ama," muttered Vic to himself. Vic shook his head to both fend off the flies that were already beginning to be annoying and to rid himself of his self-pity.

Trying to pull himself together and turning back to the task at hand, Vic resignedly walked, trotted, grazed and stumbled amongst the Zebra for what seemed like a lifetime. But, despite being safe, he was wrapped up in his problem and beating himself up for being so stupid.

Vic questioned how he could have considered venturing away when, now, he missed his mother and the rest of the Herd. When he could, he kept his eyes scanning ahead to see if there was any sign of any Wildebeest. Admittedly, at times there wasn't much more to see other than billowing dust stirred by the thousands of hooves ahead. All thoughts of adventure were now gone — now it was about the food, water and security that can only truly be found amongst your own.

Chapter Two

On the Journey, the various groupings tended to move at differing speeds whilst covering different amounts of ground each day. It was a small wonder why Vic and the group of Zebra had not come across Vic's Herd after so much time. Vic knew that he was at the mercy of the Zebras' Journey but, admittedly, he was too scared to take the risk and venture out on his own — once nearly bitten, twice shy!

Days were passing and Vic's anxiety continued to fester despite being protected amongst the Zebra. The nights were even worse as he fell to sleep remembering back to the Lions, the stampede and his own carelessness and fear.

Two ominous questions now preoccupied his thoughts on a regular basis: 'Why me?' and 'Will I ever see my mom again?'

It had now been several days since that fateful evening. Little did Vic realize that, as he awoke from his disturbed rest this brightening morning, it would be a day of great significance for him.

The sun was beginning to peer over the horizon, and those first precious rays of warmth and light were advancing across the grasslands. It seemed as if these stretching fingers of light brought with them new life. As they reached each sentinel watching over each cluster of plains game, it brought with it a gentle alarm that a new day was dawning with new hopes, new promises and new travails.

Vic stirred from his sleep to the sound of some excitement.

"A watering hole!!" one nearby Zebra exclaimed to another.

"Yes. We just got word from some passing Gazelle that there is a big watering hole ahead. We should come across it this morning!"

"Well, that's good news! To think that we can all have a long drink and, perhaps, even cool off a bit. Good news indeed."

"The Gazelle said the watering hole seems to have become a focus point, as there are several converging Herds of varying sorts all heading towards it — it sounds like it is a central gathering point before the next leg of the Journey."

With that snippet, Vic did not listen to the rest of the conversation. In almost an instant, Vic's thinking and preoccupation had transformed from despair to hope. Hope! Vic now clung to the news.

"Other Herds — perhaps one would be Wildebeest?" Vic said to himself.

And, with that thought firmly fixed in his mind, Vic sprung to his feet; already he felt more purposeful and moved towards the leading edge of the group of Zebra.

The news had already spread throughout the rest of the group and there was an expectant excitement which buzzed and resonated throughout the Herd. Foregoing the first graze of the day, the reasonably small Herd quickly got themselves organized and broke into a light trot, with their eyes and ears fixed forwards, and their nostrils flared to scoop up that first tantalizing scent of water.

The predominant thought was, "Water!" for the entire Herd — all except for Vic, who could only think about his mom.

If it were possible to see from an eagle's viewpoint on the thermals above, it would be a wondrous sight to behold, as trickles and then streams of plains animals seemingly channeled towards an unknown point ahead. Here, the ground was on a slow gradient upwards and, in the distance, the horizon seemed to have been sheared off, and packets of animals were disappearing over a rim as though they were lost from the face of the now dusty plains.

Here on the ground, the Zebra noticed the distant cries of excitement more than the exhaustion of running up the gradient. Now, the animals picked up their pace and Vic happily stretched his long legs that little bit longer. He, too, had caught completely the sounds and that alluring scent of delightful water with all its promises.

Before he knew it, Vic and the Herd had crested the brow and he couldn't help but be awed by the sight before him; if he could he would have stopped to take it all in, devouring the beauty of it. But the Herd's momentum and the pressing animals following in their wake carried him and the others over the brow and down into the teaming bowl of wildlife and water.

There were thousands of animals! All were thronging and surging around a churning basin of water. A Herd of Elephant were up to their shoulders and were playing in the deepest regions; around the entire edge there was a muddied ring, both in the water and on the ground surrounding the water — evidence of the effects of thousands of hooves kneading the earth into a dough of mud.

The latest to arrive now headed straight for the water and had to press through the milling Herds in order to find a clear path to the water's edge. Vic's group spotted a small gap down to the water and steadfastly headed toward it. Of course, Vic was carried along. To try and fight his way out (which he had tried already) only ended up in him being buffeted and bruised as the group became compressed the closer they got to the water.

The distance from where they came over the edge to the water had not seemed far to Vic. Still, it had taken longer than he thought it should have done. Then again, he was young, and his concepts of time and space were still being developed.

After what seemed ages, Vic suddenly felt his feet slow down despite his body moving ahead. He had hit the muddy rim and, before he knew it, he stumbled face-first into the water. Now he was disoriented, upside-down, and unable to see clearly. Water was filling his eyes, his nostrils, his ears and his mouth. In a panic, Vic somehow righted himself, got his hooves firmly planted in the soft mud beneath him and heaved upward.

"Aarghh!" Vic broke the surface coughing and spluttering. His eruption disturbed those animals nearest for only a moment before they resumed slaking their thirsts.

Seeing that no one appeared too interested in his situation, Vic decided he should get his fill of water too; before now, he hadn't noticed just how dehydrated he felt. After a few minutes of drinking until he was content, Vic raised his head and then took stock of his surroundings; aside from the Zebra immediately nearby, on either side of him was a mixture of Eland and Gazelle. Out in the middle the water was a small Herd of Elephant showering each other. As far as Vic could tell, the entire edge of this watering hole was constantly in flux.

And then he spotted them! Wildebeest!

Over on the far shore, almost exactly opposite from where Vic stood gaping, a Herd of Wildebeest were just approaching the shore. Vic's heart began to pound in his chest, even feeling like it had skipped a beat or two. His breathing began to quicken and his legs began to move with a mind of their own. Without thinking, Vic lunged straight ahead, too determined to reach the Herd without considering his actions, and subsequently felt his feet drop out from under him — he had hit deep water. Instinct kicked in: He began to swim or, rather, thrash as he had never swum before.

Most other animals in a similar situation would probably have thought it smarter to have backed out of the water and then proceeded to circumvent the water's edge until finally reaching the others on the opposite side. But not Vic. Sticking true to character for most calves — act first, think later — Vic took the line of least resistance; not necessarily the smartest, but the shortest and straightest route nevertheless.

Fortunately, this was a sufficiently isolated watering hole, and so there were no crocodiles to prey on his plight; had there been, Vic would have been in peril.

Realizing that he was not drowning but making awkward progress, Vic continued to kick his legs beneath and behind him, keeping his eyes firmly fixed on the shore ahead and the hope it offered. With nostrils flared and his head barely above the surface, Vic breathed in staccato bursts. He was making progress and soon the Elephant, who barely noticed him and instead created waves for him to overcome, were behind him.

It was about that time when the animals on the shore began to pay an interest in the splashing and the movement heading in their direction. At any watering hole, there can be danger from all directions, and so the disturbance which Vic was creating caused some alarm; some of the animals even pulled back from the water's edge. As they did, a part in their ranks formed and there, standing watchfully still, towered one of the biggest and grandest Wildebeest Vic had ever seen. Not taking his eyes off the striking bull, Vic continued his valiant progress. Indeed, the bull had fixed Vic with a stare too.

Soon after, Vic's feet struck the bottom; the water was becoming shallow, and he was nearing the edge — he was nearing the Herd. With a mixture of both excitement and fatigue, Vic waded ashore, panting and trying hard to steady his trembling legs. Slowly, he walked hesitantly now towards the bull, who had still not moved.

"Please, Sir, can you help me?" Vic pleaded.

Silence.

"I lost my mom several days ago; that is, I got separated from my mom, my friend, Ama, and my Herd when some Lion attacked," Vic blurted out. "I have been traveling for days with a group of kindly Zebra. When we got here, on the other side of this watering hole, I saw this group of Wildebeest and thought you might be able to help. I thought you might know my mom?"

Silence.

Barely noticeable, the bull's eyes slowly scanned left to right and then up and down. Vic now felt as if he was being examined in detail — sized-up — and the verdict was imminent.

Vic recalled somewhat belatedly an early lesson his mother had given to him: "Vic, when dealing with bulls, always wait to be spoken to first."

He realized it would now be very prudent to now show respect and to wait. His guts told him this was a significant moment.

After some time had passed, the bull finally spoke. "What is your name?"

"Vic, Sir," Vic quietly replied.

"Who is your mother?"

"Moh, Sir."

"Hmm. There is no cow in our Herd with that name."

Up to this point since arriving ashore, Vic had been alive and vibrant with adrenaline coursing through every artery and vein of his body. Now, Vic felt his heart and spirit plummet. And, as if his body heard his heart begin to shatter, his head started to droop and his ears to wilt.

After a pregnant pause, the bull continued, "We cannot have you go it alone looking for your mother. You will join us, and you will stick close to me. After all, any calf — foolhardy and, yet, resilient enough to survive Lion and to travel days without the Herd and to swim uncharted waters — at least has some potential." The bull made his point emphatically before asking, "Do you understand, young calf?"

"Yes, Sir." Vic replied.

"Stop calling me 'Sir' — you may call me Men-taur."

And with that, the bull turned and headed away from the water. The other wildebeest that stood by his side also turned and followed after having to press forward against the tide of animals who were heading for an urgently needed drink.

"Hey, kid!" One of them blew as he brushed past, spraying Vic with a mixture of water, spit and mud.

This startled Vic as he had been rooted to the spot. He wasn't exactly sure why; any other animal looking his way would have thought he was dumb-struck. His jaw was open, his tongue lolled from the corner of his mouth and he looked forward with a fixed stare.

"I'd stop gawking and start walking if I were you. Unless you want to get lost again or, worse, get on the wrong side of Men-taur," added the same Beest over his pronounced shoulders, as he proceeded up through the closing throng.

And then, to emphasize his point further, Vic heard a bellow from somewhere ahead (but not too far), "Vic! Are you coming?!"

Vic needed no further encouragement. He sprang forth and followed close on the heels of the last Beest, wading through the crowd.

Shortly, the crowd appeared to thin and Vic was able to see amidst the tangle of legs ahead and around him some increasing patches of grassy space. And then, suddenly he was free, no longer having to stare at the swishing tail of the Beest in front, as open space appeared before him.

And there before Vic, centered in his line of sight, stood a towering Men-taur looking menacing with his polished horns that seemed etched with the fire of the reflected sunlight. Vic hesitated a step as he caught a searching look from the eyes of Men-taur.

"Well? Hurry up, Vic!" Men-taur urged with a tinge of impatience.

"Y-y-yes, Sir! I mean Men-taur," Vic stammered.

As the other Beests continued on ahead, Men-taur waited until Vic came alongside before turning to follow. Vic was, it seemed, the last animal in the line.

"Walk beside me." It was neither a request nor a statement. It just, well, was.

Little did Vic realize what an honor this simple allowance was; rarely were new calves asked to walk alongside a bull, let alone orphans. Even more amazing was the fact that Men-taur was the head of this Herd (as Vic would soon find out). Heads were usually loners and took few other Beests' counsel or suffered fools. Men-taur, however, was different, as Vic would find out over the days, weeks and months ahead.

"Okay, Vic. Tell me your full story."

This was less a request and more an expectation. Vic did not hesitate, and filled the next hour or so by recounting his trials and tribulations of his Journey so far. He sensed he had better stick to the basics and keep any embellishments from his story; only once did he start to go off track but a snort from Men-taur brought him up short and sharp. Clearly, Men-taur had his limits. Almost throughout his entire monologue Vic noted that all Men-taur did was listen or acknowledge with the odd snort or grunt at a particular point. Only on a few occasions did he interject with a very targeted question for clarification.

At about the time he finished, Vic realized that it was becoming darker with the onset of dusk. There was perhaps about an hour's worth of daylight remaining. As the Herd had collectively walked, they had grazed on the occasional patch of short grass that Beests, like them, preferred. Now, the air was cooling, and the soundscape was transitioning from day to night with an increase in the volume of crickets, cicadas and other insects and a decrease in the lowing of the Herd. The animals around them were beginning to slow and settle in groups across the expanse of the valley.

An expanse it most certainly was. The Herd rested on a gentle decline and, from his vantage point, Vic could see a Herd of thousands milling about. The sheer size of it awed Vic. He stopped in his tracks; Men-taur didn't.

He turned — or at least his head did.

"You stay here with the others," directed Men-taur. "You seemed to have picked a good vantage point for me to watch over the Herd. Well done. I need to go ahead and speak to a few others about setting up for the night. We need to make sure we have sentries alert for the dangers that will surely be out there in this night. I'll be back," Men-taur added reassuringly.

Vic didn't need any imagination to know what Men-taur meant when referring to dangers. There were the all-too-familiar Lion. But then there were the Hyena and the Leopard, and the Vulture which would surely follow the seeking Herds, waiting to target any loosely wandering victim. The thought of the hunters caused a chill to run down Vic's spine, and his mane trembled with the last vestiges of the thought. He cast his eyes around him to identify the nearest group of Beest.

There was a large group of about fifty or more only about thirty paces away. They were already settling in their lines for the night, so Vic trotted over.

"Excuse me. May I join you, please?" Vic asked of a nearby cow who was busy licking her calf's haunches.

Vic's mother had always told him from the very moment he took his first breath that it was always wise to be polite. He could hear her now saying, "Courtesy costs nothing; it is a great investment in your future."

"Yes, of course," the cow motioned with her muzzle, interrupting Vic's recollection, "You may lay down next to us."

"Men-taur suggested I settle for the night around here."

"You are traveling with Men-taur?" queried the cow.

"Yes," Vic nodded for emphasis.

"My word! That is most unusual. Then again, nothing about Men-taur is usual. He is one-of-a-kind," she replied with both surprise and bemusement. And, with that, she turned back to her calf.

Vic looked around for a comparatively soft place to lie down upon the baked earth. Once he was satisfied he had found just such a spot, he circled once and then dropped. As he did so, he became aware of how sore and how tired he was; even his throat was raw and aching. His last drink had been at the watering hole, and even then he had been talking and breathing in dust for the remainder of the day.

Now he had time to reflect.

*Courtesy costs nothing; it is a great
investment in your future.*

While he had not yet found his mother, Vic knew he had to acknowledge what had he so far achieved: He had returned to his own kind, and had also been blessed to have been invited to join a new Herd by its leader — an iconic bull who emanated power, authority and, strangely (well, at least to Vic), compassion.

As Vic took stock of his day, darkness fully took over the Serengeti, and the air quickly cooled. Vic's mind wrestled for a little longer over what had happened over the past several days before surrendering to sleep. As he did so a large dark shape seemingly hovered over him briefly.

Under the pale soft light of the moon, a small grin broke across Men-taur's face. "Sleep well. You will find what you are looking for and then some. The way will not be easy, but you will grow."

Men-taur hovered a moment longer and then disappeared, blending into the night.

Chapter Three

The next day dawned as most days did now: Hot and dry. What this meant to the myriad Herds spread across the land was the further urge to press on with this annual migration; at this time of year, good grazing was decreasing as the Herds passed through. In addition, the watering holes were becoming smaller with what seemed to be greater distances between them. This combination created the innate need and primal drive for the animals to continue on with their daily quest for food and water — and that was exactly what Men-taur had in mind when Vic woke up.

Noting Vic's stirring and bleary eyes, Men-taur stated, "Vic, the time has come for the Herd to move on. Time waits for no Beest. I need to guide the Herd to find water and better grazing. Join me. You will learn something new today."

Men-taur then trotted off away from the rising sun, with his head fixed on some undisclosed point ahead of him. Vic barely had the time to grab a quick nibble of grass as he hastily pulled himself to his feet, cleared the lingering sleepiness, and headed off at a canter to catch up.

When Vic finally reached his leader's side, Men-taur turned his head and nodded, then resumed his fixed distance look. After several minutes, Men-taur broke the silence. "What do you know about the Journey?"

By now they had slowed their pace so Vic could reply without having to juggle breathing with speaking as he had the day before. "I know only what my mother told me, that it happens every year and is part of the Way of Things," Vic replied obediently.

"Well, it's time to enhance your education, Vic. So be sure to listen," Men-taur emphasized. "The Journey has been taking place here on the Land for many years and many more seasons — it is all part of the Circle of Life. Just like the celestial bodies above — the stars, moon and sun — follow their own path across the seasons and years, so too does life here on the plains and amongst us Wildebeest." Men-taur looked up to the sky momentarily before continuing. "It is said that once, at some time in our ancestors' past, the Journey did not exist. It was during this time that the Earth was abundant — teaming with life; from the Termite to the Elephant and the grass to the Acacia Tree, water and foliage were always in good supply. And then, Vic, something changed in the lands — whether it was a small or big change or a series of changes, we do not know, but the change just happened. Suddenly, the rains did not come as often or as much; the grass therefore grew and then stopped, and this became the Way of Things and gave life to the Journey."

Vic continued to walk by Men-taur's side, mesmerized by how he spoke and his vast knowledge on things Vic had only ever taken for granted.

"The Journey is one of survival, Vic. It is a game, almost — survival of the fittest. Each year, each one of us follow a Circle — a Journey with no beginning and no end; it is an endless quest for water and food — not just for Wildebeest but for all wildlife here on the plains. Each year, we cover vast distances which consist of an endless horizon and an infinite number of paces. We follow a pattern. Usually the Zebra precede us and the Elephant and Gazelle follow us. Because we spread out for great distances, this order is often not obvious but each animal group has its own order and pace with their own way of approaching the Journey. We Wildebeest are, by far, the largest group. Each year, our numbers bloom up to one and a half million, although on the Journey we lose up to one sixth of our number amongst the sick, the lame, the injured and, like you, Vic, the young. It is important each one of us realize, you see, that dangers exist along the way: There are the Lion and Hyena, to name a minority; a few which are sent to test our limits and to take from our numbers. Nature's forces claim their fair share. Stampedes take considerable numbers."

Vic was, by now, walking by his mentor's side with his head down, listening to the wise bull's words while admiring each individual blade they walked across, marveling at all that Nature puts each living thing through in the survival of the fittest.

"The Journey asks of us all that we strike a balance with all other forces. Each type of animal is attuned to its part of the Journey, and so long as we stay in harmony with our part of the Journey, all will remain well. Indeed, only a select few animals amongst the diverse types within the Journey are highly attuned to the Rhythm." Men-taur paused for a moment. "You do know about the Rhythm, Vic?"

Vic raised his head and met Men-taur's strong gaze and shook his head warily, unsure as to whether this was something he should have known the answer to.

Men-taur nodded and continued. "The Rhythm, Vic, is the pulse of the Circle of Life. It acts as a guide for all life who are synchronized to its cadence. These attuned animals often rise to leadership in their respective Herds and packs. They ensure the balance is maintained, the Circle of Life is played out, and the Journey continues. Fortunately, Vic, I am one such animal; I have been blessed since the day I was born with the Rhythm within — my own father imparted to me the wisdom of the Journey and, Vic, I sense that the Rhythm is within you, too."

Vic stared up at Men-taur, shocked by his revelation, and somehow feeling undeserving of such a statement.

"Note, Vic, that there are seven lessons my father taught me to help me harness the Rhythm and to become a true success of myself and the life with which the Earth has blessed me. These seven success factors are simple and, yet, profound. In isolation they do not amount to much; in combination, however, their synergy brings to life all that is possible when you believe. So Vic," finished Men-taur, "you have a choice: To stay on your current path and search for your mother or to become a student of the Rhythm. This is your choice."

Once again, Vic found himself caught up in his own thoughts as he reflected on what Men-taur had been saying. Suddenly, he noticed that he was creating a widening gulf between Men-taur's challenge and his own answer. Suddenly, feeling uncomfortable with the silence, Vic made the most significant decision of his short life.

"Yes, I do," he replied somewhat euphorically. "I want to become a student of the Rhythm and become a success."

Chapter Four

"Each goal has a destination and a Journey. You must learn to thrive to arrive. Remember that where you are going and how you get there are two totally different things. Regrettably, many focus on the destination and not the Journey and, therefore, never reach the destination."

Bob Gass

"Individuals can live without certainty from a leader, but not without clarity."

John C Maxwell

Once again, Vic found himself facing an unsettling silence as he waited for Men-taur to respond. The seconds seemed like minutes until, finally, Men-taur nodded and affirmed, "Well done. You have made a very wise choice. Now, before you begin to live the lessons that I will pass on to you, we need to establish some ground rules," Men-taur continued. "Over the course of our Journey during this Circle, I will educate you in the seven lessons. At the conclusion of our time, I expect you to be as fully versed in the Rhythm as I am; however, note that I expect that this will only become a starting point for you Vic," emphasized Men-taur, "For with each generation, the knowledge of the Rhythm is expected to grow, for what does not grow dies. You must understand, Vic, that with growth comes a responsibility to share its fruits; only by sharing does true abundance flow."

For what does not grow dies. With growth comes a responsibility to share its fruits; only by sharing does true abundance flow.

"So first, as your lessons ensue, I expect you to be prepared where applicable, and on time, where appointed. Please ask questions; only by asking good questions do you truly learn and gain useful knowledge pertinent to you. But please know, Vic, I am not preventing you from enjoying the vibrancy of youth — life is to be experienced in its fullness and its greatness; not just at the feet of an old bull."

"Now, being prepared includes not only any work you have agreed to have ready, but also includes coming with the right attitude — an expectant one." Men-taur then added, "This way, you'll gain the most value and focus from our times together. Vic, it will help you if you see these sessions as an island of focus and calm in the middle of the hardship of the Journey."

Men-taur then looked down at his young apprentice. "Understood?" asked Men-taur rhetorically.

Vic was taking two steps for every one of Men-taur's, and it was apparent Vic was attentively listening.

Only by asking good questions do you truly learn and gain useful knowledge pertinent to you.

"Good. Secondly, at the end of each session, you will be asked to summarize your learning and, where necessary, your commitments. This will allow you to consolidate your learning and clarify your commitments upon which you will be focused until the next session. Note, Vic, that this also helps me to check your understanding of the lesson and lets me know what I need to monitor and follow-up with you," finished Men-taur.

Without any need for prompting, Vic added an emphatic, "Understood."

Vic was keen to absorb every nuance and nugget of the wisdom that Men-taur chose to pass onto him.

"Hhhmmph!" snorted Men-taur.

Vic winced. He quickly realized that, perhaps, he should measure his responses and his timing of them; already, he was beginning to grasp that Men-taur did not tolerate rash and reckless behavior in any shape or form.

Turning his head once again so that he could look fixedly into Vic's eyes, Men-taur exhaled slowly and with control stated, "Right, thirdly, there are consequences for any lack of attention and preparation. For the first transgression, I will ask you for a suitable consequence that you believe you should assume." After one of those now tell-tale pauses, Men-taur continued, "A second means I will come up with the consequence." With an even more penetrating gaze, Men-taur finished, "In the very unlikely event of a third, the session and future sessions will be terminated. Is that clear?"

"Yes, Sir. I mean Men-taur," Vic replied, correcting himself under Men-taur's gaze.

"Any questions?" Men-taur asked.

"No, Men-taur." Vic replied.

Men-taur suddenly turned his head to gaze off into the distance ahead. Shortly, he turned his attention back to Vic and added a quick, "Good." Then, as if considering something, Men-taur added, "It's now time for me to see to my duties. Grazing and water in this area are generally pocketed at this time of year; I need to confer with others. So we will have to leave your first lesson until tomorrow, first light." Men-taur took his first few steps forward and then turned to Vic. "So, Vic, when are we next meeting?" asked Men-taur, in-line with the ground rules.

"First light tomorrow, Sir."

Hearing the right response Men-taur nodded, shook his mane forcefully to dislodge some irritating flies, and then trotted off.

Vic felt a vacuum now that Men-taur had gone; how he longed to join Men-taur. He sensed that when the time was right, he would be invited along but, for now, he had to curb this desire.

Before long, Vic was wondering what the first lesson was going to be; that then became the predominant thought in Vic's mind as he gamboled off excitedly to find another group of calves playing nearby. He only took breaks to graze when his stomachs told him he was hungry.

As with most days, the Herd finished its day near to a watering hole. As Beest generally drink twice a day, this strategy made sense; with each successive day on the Journey, they would only need to actually find one new watering hole each day.

At the end of another long day, all the various Herds seemed to segregate and settle down. As was the standard practice, a few select individuals were posted at key vantage points around and amongst the Herd with the responsibility of maintaining watch for any predators or other dangers. At night all senses were heightened, and the so-called sentries allowed the rest of the Herd to relax with an expectant contentment that, should the need arise, a timely alarm would be sounded.

Vic, having only learned of this practice today, nestled reassuredly down in the grass amongst some of his new friends and their mothers.

The next thing Vic knew, he was being nudged awake by a nearby mother who was simultaneously feeding her calf. All around, Vic noticed the preparations for the new day on the Journey. Fortunately, preparations always preceded first light; pre-dawn was, after all, a favorite time for lions to attack the Herd.

With growling stomachs, Vic quickly grabbed a few mouthfuls of grass and scanned around and ahead of him to determine where to find Men-taur. He did not have to search long; there was a small knoll nearby outlined with a nimbus of light predicting the coming sunlight and there, on its top, Vic could make out the unmistakable grand figure of Men-taur.

Vic headed toward the knoll. As he approached, Men-taur turned his far-off gaze down toward Vic. "Good Morning, Vic," stated Men-taur.

"Good Morning, Men-taur," replied Vic.

"Join me," said Men-taur, halfway between a request and a command.

Vic approached and drew alongside Men-taur.

Maintaining his gaze toward where the sun will set that day, Men-taur asked, "What do you see, Vic?"

Vic stared out in the same direction. In reply, Vic responded, "I see the Herd beginning to get ready for the day. From here I see that some are heading down to the watering hole for their first drink; others are beginning to graze and the calves are getting their first milk of the day."

"Look further," Men-taur continued.

After casting about his head and straining his eyes for a few moments, Vic continued. "Well I can just begin to make out some Zebra up ahead who are already heading off for the day. By the sounds of things — although I can't see them yet — there are also some Elephant approaching the watering hole from the direction we came yesterday."

"What else?" Men-taur prompted.

"I don't really see anything else yet, Men-taur. There is not enough light for me to see much further," Vic said with a hint of frustration.

"I do not expect you to be able to answer my initial questions fully. Remember that," Men-taur began, "And, importantly, don't allow yourself the feeling of frustration; you are learning."

And then, as if almost on-cue, Nature answered Men-taur's question: The first rays of sunlight flowed warmly past them and brightened the landscape ahead of them; it was as if the sunlight knew where it was headed and was already stretching towards the place where it would set at day's end.

"Okay, Vic, now what do you see?" asked Men-taur.

"Well, I can certainly see more clearly. The grassland reaches out far ahead of us and is spotted with acacia trees. There is Gazelle raising some billows of dust; they are running and leaping ahead with a few lions in pursuit," Vic finished with a concerned expression on his face.

Men-taur added, "Yes, but what is beyond all of this? Look as far as you can see. You have young eyes so you should be able to see beyond what I can."

Vic's brow was furrowed as he turned from listening to Men-taur to looking ahead once again. Now, somewhat unsure of himself, Vic offered, "Well, I can only see to a point where it all becomes a blur and indistinct — where the sky meets the ground."

"Exactly!" exclaimed Men-taur. "That leads nicely into your first lesson on success as a leader. Vision. What you just described, Vic — where the ground meets the sky — is what is known as the Horizon," stated Men-taur. "As a leader, it is crucially important to set your sights on the Horizon. Why do you think that is, Vic?"

Vic answered , "So that I am able to see what is ahead of me."

Lesson 1 - Vision

"Yes, that is true, but is still only part of the full answer," Men-taur responded. "The Horizon, you see, may appear the same as always but, in fact, is actually always changing: What was before us yesterday is different to what is before us today. There are new grasslands, new watering holes, new dangers, new opportunities, new decisions... Now, a question, Vic: What does the Horizon look like for that Beest down there?" Men-taur asked, indicating with his left fore-hoof towards an old bull at the foot of the knoll.

"Well," started Vic, "he won't be able to see what we see from up here. If I were where he is, all I would see would be a forest of Beest round about me."

> What was before us yesterday is
> different to what is before us today.

"Correct." Men-taur agreed. "The Horizon does look different for each and every one of us and, for some, like you and that old bull, you cannot even see the Horizon because you are too mixed up in the daily wear and tear of the Circle of Life." Men-taur paused to let the notion sink in before continuing. "In order to gain a true perspective on the Horizon, it is always important to find a good vantage point from which to look at it and to study it. In fact, before we proceed, why would you want to study the Horizon?"

Before responding, Vic took some time to think. Men-taur waited patiently. Finally, Vic answered, "To see what lies ahead."

"Right again. Well done, Vic." Men-taur said encouragingly. "When a leader knows what lies ahead, it gives them time to plan the route and, where necessary, to make any changes — big or small — to the plan so, while the Journey follows the same general path each year, it is never the exact same path; things change and we must adapt." Men-taur paused for a while, enabling Vic to look around him and to get a feel for the teachings. "Each day," Men-taur continued, "I make sure that I begin and end the day from the best vantage point. I begin the day scanning the Horizon to establish what changes have occurred since I last scanned it the night before and, where possible, I will make the time and effort throughout the day and at other key times and points along the Journey to gain a vantage point and check that progress is being made according to what I envision is best for the Herd."

As Men-taur appeared to have stopped, Vic asked, "Does everyone have to see the Horizon?"

"A good question," answered Men-taur. "Everyone who wants to truly succeed must have their own Horizon in mind; without it, they could simply end up wandering aimlessly with no direction and fall prey to the predators that look out for such unsuspecting and unprepared victims. The Horizon naturally ties in to the key point of this lesson — your Vision," stated Men-taur. "From my experience, here in the Circle of Life, those who truly resonate with the Rhythm and the success it provides have this as one of the seven key attributes," continued Men-taur. "A strong Vision allows a Beest — or any other animal, for that matter — to always maintain a sense of perspective and a point of reference for all attitudes, decisions and actions. Your Vision must be so strong and so compelling that it ultimately provides you with energy and momentum at all times, especially when things perhaps get a little tough — as we would all expect them to be." Men-taur paused a moment before adding, "Another way of describing your Vision is that it is your overall view of things for your life — its pinnacle. Your vision, Vic, will be yours and, where relevant, as you grow, others — likely those who abide less in the flow of the Rhythm — will capture your Vision and join you. Does that make sense so far, Vic?"

"I think so," Vic replied with a hint of uncertainty.

Men-taur picked up on this and offered, "Well, perhaps some examples may help."

"Yes. That would be good."

"Okay then," acknowledged Men-taur. "Take my leading this Herd. The Herd is trusting me to get as many of them as possible through the Journey this year, and for me to do so as safely as possible. As part of that expectation and my own responsibility, I am to lead them in such a way that ensures there is always enough to eat and drink each day."

Men-taur paused. Seeing that Vic did not have any questions at this point, he continued. "With that in mind, I have a Vision of what my outcome will be when we have completed this Journey; it is my absolute ideal. I keep that picture firmly in my mind at all times and, in particular, I focus on that image and ruminate on it at least twice a day — first thing in the morning and last thing at night. I picture it; I think about it and clarify how it will make me feel when I achieve it. It becomes a point of reference. By doing all of this gives me greater clarity as I lead along the Journey. So far, each Journey I have led has ended up almost exactly as I had envisioned it. Understand, Vic that, where you have clarity you have greater power to achieve your success."

Before Men-taur could go on, Vic asked, "How do I go about creating my Vision?"

"Another good question," Men-taur assured. "Remember, I mentioned the importance of you having a good vantage point?"

> Where you have clarity you have greater
> power to achieve your success.

"Yes," nodded Vic.

"Well, let's look at another example that will be of help," Men-taur suggested. "Look up in the sky over there," Men-taur indicated with his muzzle off to their left. Vic turned his eyes to follow Men-taur's gaze. "Do you see that Eagle aloft riding on the wind?" asked Men-taur.

Once again, Vic nodded.

"Well, that Eagle is designed to fly and to do so effortlessly by soaring on the wind and the rising banks of heated air from the ground below," Men-taur explained. "Interestingly," Men-taur emphasized, "that Eagle has a unique view on what is going on around us; Eagles actually have perfect vision. At any one time their eyes are in perfect focus. Unlike us we can only focus on what is before us with everything to the sides in our peripheral vision being less clear. Well, everything that Eagle sees is seen with perfect clarity; this allows it to scan and detect danger and prey without haziness in its entire field of view."

"Wow! Really?" exclaimed Vic.

"Indeed," acknowledged Men-taur. "That Eagle — like you, Vic — has been created and designed to fulfil its niche in the Circle of Life; each of us has a purpose and each of us is fit for purpose. "However," Men-taur asserted, "not every animal even considers such a profound matter; it is those who don't who tend to fall into the role of being followers; those who do consider such wondrous things do tend to be leaders." Men-taur looked down at the young calf and continued. "That Eagle, like its kind, knows why it is here, joining us on the Journey on the Circle of Life. It knows its purpose is to survive, to overcome adversity, and to help its offspring to get the best start in life. This then perpetuates their species to the next generation and beyond."

Vic continued to watch the eagle, considering the wisdom of Men-taur's words, desperately trying to log each point into his mind.

"In fact, Vic, each and every living thing has a purpose. For example," continued Men-taur, "the grass shelters the Ant and the Termite, and they in turn help to bind the soil. We, in turn, eat the grass, which helps us to grow and gives us the energy we require to fulfil our purpose on the Journey. Everything created is an answer to someone or something else's needs. It is, therefore, worth asking yourself, Vic, 'Whose needs do I choose to fulfil?'"

Men-taur turned to look expectantly at Vic.

Vic, still staring at the circling eagle, was so absorbed in what Men-taur was teaching him, he had not noticed that Men-taur had actually stopped.

"Ahhem!" Men-taur loudly and purposefully cleared his throat.

Vic, startled, shook his head almost imperceptibly and apologized, "Sorry, Men-taur. I was trying to listen to what you were saying and to understand what it must be like to be an Eagle and to be able to see everything all at once with the same focus."

Men-taur smiled momentarily and tolerantly requested, "So, what is the answer? Whose needs do you choose to fulfil?"

"I suppose it's down, in part, to my preferences," Vic suggested.

"What do you mean?" queried Men-taur.

"Well, at the moment I do not see myself fulfilling anyone's needs, although I am sure the Lion, the ticks and the flies would offer that I fulfil their need." Vic said.

"Okay, that's good," Men-taur agreed with a smile.

"My preference, I suppose, is much like the Eagle, which is to fulfil the need of eventually adding to our numbers and continuing the Herd. From what you said to me yesterday, Men-taur, you say I have the potential to fulfil the Rhythm and, hopefully, one day, lead the Herd," Vic concluded.

"Very good," Men-taur nodded approvingly.

> Everything created is an answer to someone or something else's needs.

By now, the entire Herd had awoken and were heading toward the Horizon which had been the starting point of Vic's first lesson. The sun was fully paving the way ahead to the accompaniment of a vast array of wildlife on both the wind and ground that were following its bright trail to the promises of a new day.

Now beginning to head down off the knoll with Vic eagerly alongside, Men-taur took a slow, deep breath through flared nostrils, exhaled just as slowly, and then continued, "I think this makes a convenient point for us to conclude your lesson on this first success factor — having a strong and compelling Vision. So, as a summary, please could you recap the key points, Vic, of what we have covered?"

Vic took a moment to consider all of his leader's teachings, and replayed as much of his knowledge and wisdom as he could remember. Taking a deep breath, Vic began, "Today, you helped me to understand that, firstly, my Horizon is always changing." Vic looked up at Men-taur for approval, but continued when he was met with silence. "Secondly, you taught me of the importance of securing a good vantage point from which I can observe and study my Horizon. Thirdly, I must have a strong and compelling Vision for my life, which will help me maintain a sense of perspective. My Vision will give me a point of reference for all my attitudes, decisions and actions. For my Vision to be clear, I must first consider my Vision at least twice a day." Vic stopped for a moment to think and ensure he had missed nothing before finishing. "And, finally, to help me to understand how to go about creating my Vision, I must first understand my purpose in the Circle of Life. I must ask myself whose needs I need to fulfil; when I know that answer, it will be easier for me to then create and contemplate my Vision as it fits my purpose," concluded Vic.

"Excellent, Vic," affirmed Men-taur with a modest nod. "Now, until we next meet, I suggest you give some very serious thought and consideration to each of the key points we have addressed and, most importantly, put them into practice; I want you to look within you and fathom what the Rhythm is telling you. At our next meeting you will be able to tell me briefly what your own Vision is. Understood?"

"Yes, Men-taur," Vic nodded emphatically.

With that, Men-taur broke into a trot. And, like responding to a silent alarm, the Beest nearby began to part. With his words being carried back to Vic on the now strengthening breeze, Men-taur finished, "Remember to work on this every day. I'll let you know when the time has come for your next lesson."

And then, in the quickest of moments, Men-taur was gone and the Herd had closed around him.

Vic felt strange and yet nevertheless excited; strange because he already missed Men-taur; excited because he was eager to put things into practice and determine what his Vision was.

"You are what the Creator says you are. You have what the Creator says you have, therefore, you can do what the Creator says you can do. So stop, look and listen to what the Land reveals to you."

Anonymous

"Imagination is more important than knowledge. For knowledge is limited to all we now know and understand, while imagination embraces the entire world, and all there ever will be to know and understand."

Albert Einstein

Exercise 1 - Your Vision

Please consider this exercise very carefully and thoughtfully, as it pertains to any one of the following: Your life, your purpose, your career, your family, your business, your sport, your role and/or your goal.

So, in relation to one or more of the above

1.   Write down your Vision concisely and clearly:

_____

_____

_____

2.   Using a rating scale of 1-10*, _____
      how strong is your Vision?

3.   In the event that you scored yourself below an 8,
      what 3 things do you need to be and/or do which
      will contribute to increasing the power of your
      Vision to an 8+?

_____

_____

_____

_____

_____

_____

_____

_____

_____

* For this and the other exercises, please note that a score of 1 represents the weakest and a score of 10 represents the strongest.

Chapter Five

"Man is so made that when anything fires his soul, impossibilites vanish."

Jean De La Fountaine

*"A warrior doesn't give up what he loves...
he finds the love in what he does."*

Socrates

Several days had passed. Vic couldn't be sure exactly how many as he had become caught up in the daily pattern of the Herd and his own thoughts about his Vision. During that period, he had only seen Men-taur fleetingly. Vic stayed in the central part of the Herd, partly because that was where the nursery groups and orphans traveled, and partly because of his previous experience of going beyond the Edge the night he became separated from his mother.

Vic had found some other orphans within the Herd, and he had chosen to play with those youngsters; they had that one core fact — albeit a sad one — in common. That fact helped to numb some of the pain and sense of loss each one had felt, but none of the orphans discussed it. Instead, they silently let their common ground add to the strengthening of their kinship and, as a result, they began to spend all their time outside of playtime together. They grazed, slept, ruminated and drank together.

Today had seemed a normal enough day. But, as the Herd grazed through the landscape, Vic began to notice some changes around him — within the Herd and without. First, it seemed the air was getting dustier; indeed, everywhere Vic looked — whether from a vantage point or not (he had heeded Men-taur's first lesson well) — there were perpetual clouds of dust that had been kicked up and kept up by the passing animals. Amidst the dust the landscape was changing with an increasing mixture of acacia woodlands and savannah, and it was perhaps this which had led to his other observation.

Vic noticed also that the Herd seemed to be thinning out. This morning, Vic had climbed atop a small rock outcrop and had scanned his Horizon. From that position, he had noted that the Herd had become stretched out ahead, and were also moving in the direction from which they had already come; in fact, he had noticed that it seemed like one part of the Herd was veering off in a different direction. This thought had been perplexing him all day. Vic had just stopped to contemplate it again.

The sun was now more clearly ahead of him as it began its descent from its daily apex. Vic was just lowering his eyes from the relentlessness of the sun's bright, penetrating rays when that same light was cut off by a looming shadow. Through slitted eyes, Vic looked back up, and there stood Men-taur.

This time, he appeared different. It was only when Men-taur shook his mane and the red clinging dust rose around him that Vic understood why; the dust had blanketed Men-taur and, as he looked around, blanketed mostly everyone and everything — moving and still.

Now, Vic took all of this in within a moment because, blowing his nostrils, Men-taur spoke. "Good day, Vic! How are you today?"

"Fine, thank you Men-taur," answered Vic. "Well, I would be if it were not for all this dust and the fact that everything I eat, including my cud, takes like dirt," answered Vic.

"Huh!" grunted Men-taur. "I know what you mean. A little rain to wash away the dirt and to dampen the dust would be just the thing right now."

Vic felt a little warmth flow through him as he realized Men-taur was not only wise and disciplined, but also humorous and light-hearted on occasion.

"I regret I have not been able to meet up with you over the past several days," Men-taur said, interrupting Vic's thoughts. "There have been... other pressing matters. These past couple of days we have been harried by some Hyena and finding food and water is becoming increasingly more difficult. But, now that things seem to be settling down," assured Men-taur, "I can give you some time so that we can progress your education on the Rhythm, the Journey, success and leadership."

Vic smiled and shifted happily from hoof to hoof, before composing himself.

"Are you ready to begin your second lesson, Vic?"

After another, almost characteristic pause, Vic acknowledged definitively, "Yes, Men-taur!"

"Good. Now, before we progress, what were my parting words to you when we last spoke?" asked Men-taur.

Men-taur had now moved aside to bring himself alongside Vic. Looking upward at Men-taur, Vic responded, "I was to keep in mind and apply the key points regarding having a Vision as a leader. You had also asked me to come up with my own Vision and be prepared to share it with you."

"Yes, that's right," snorted Men-taur, and then continued, "Now, before we progress to our second lesson, I want you to remember that your Vision is just that — yours. No one else will have your exact Vision; they might catch it, align to it and even adopt it, but it will not be their Vision. They may, however, integrate it into their own to help strengthen theirs. For instance, my Vision is to lead the Herd for as many Journeys as I can whilst ensuring the best and safest routes where food and water are in abundant supply. And, similarly, the male leading a pride of Lions will have his own Vision for their part of the Journey. The common denominator is the Journey, regardless of species, and comes before all else. The Journey is, after all, the Way of Things; the way everything becomes interlinked so that all life joins together. Does that make sense, Vic?" finished Men-taur.

"Yes. Everything is inextricably linked so that your Vision, my Vision and a Lion's Vision become interdependent."

"Exactly. Well done, Vic," said Men-taur, clearly impressed.

Men-taur waited a moment before asking, "So, Vic, what is your Vision?"

"I want to be—", Vic began but, before he could continue, Men-taur interrupted.

"Vic, remember — you don't have to share your Vision with me. As you may recall, I did say that you should be prepared to share it; that is not to say you are required to share it. Only share your Vision with those who you wish to entrust it to for they will be the ones who will help you achieve it with their support, encouragement, resources and ideas. I don't share my Vision with the male Lion because I am guessing his Vision may run in contrast to mine, and also because he poses a critical risk to my Vision."

Men-taur stopped. Vic considered what Men-taur had just said and then asked, "Men-taur, can I ask then why you shared your Vision with me?"

"Good question," replied Men-taur, "The short answer is because you are in my Herd for which I am responsible and I believe you have the makings of leading this Herd. Also, you would not fully understand what Vision is if I didn't give you a good example." Men-taur finished off his reply with a wink.

Vic giggled. "Oh. Well, I do want to tell you my Vision."

The two were just reaching an opening in the savannah from where they could see the land starting to slope down away from them; it was almost as if the land was underlining this moment by giving them both a vantage point to survey what was before them. The significance was not lost on Vic.

Vic spoke out, as if to everyone and yet, most importantly to himself. "Just as I can now see above the various Herds and groupings ahead as they are mixed in with the dust, I picture leading the Herd — like you, Men-taur — improving on what you have achieved and establishing a School of Success where the leaders and future leaders from every grazing and foraging animal here on the Journey can work together to improve the Circle of Life."

"Well done, Vic. Well done," Men-taur nodded approvingly with his lower lip jutting out.

Up until this point, Vic had only really thought about this, and so this was the first time he had spoken about his Vision aloud. As he did so, he had felt himself grow; it was like the land was filling him up from the ground, pouring its energy into him. Everything seemed to grow clearer, and everything was in a keener focus.

With his Vision shared, Men-taur enlightened Vic, "To speak your Vision is to give it life. To speak it with Passion is to give it power! And that, Vic," continued Men-taur, "leads nicely into your next lesson. The second attribute of success is Passion."

> *To speak your vision is to give it life.*
> *To speak it with Passion is to give it power!*

"Okay Vic, what is Passion? How would you describe it?" started Men-taur.

"Well, I think Passion is about putting all of your energy into something," replied Vic, with a somewhat puzzled look on his face.

Noting Vic's puzzlement, Men-taur added reassuringly, "In part, Vic, you are on the right track."

Lesson 2 - Passion

That did not help Vic at all. He looked expectantly towards Men-taur who obligingly began to explain, "Passion is being consumed with a powerful emotion or feeling. Or, another way of describing it is as a compelling desire for something — something physical, a goal, a time, another creature of this world. What it is bears little or no significance — the feeling of Passion that spurs you on is what matters." After a brief pause to determine that Vic was following what he was saying, Men-taur continued, "In short, Vic, to be successful means that you must have an all-consuming desire for what you are doing."

Vic nodded as he listened once again to Men-taur's wisdom.

"Can you think of an example, Vic, where you would need an all-consuming desire to achieve something?" asked Men-taur, gently hoping that Vic would make the connection that he was thinking about.

"Ummm..." Vic began and then finished with an emphatic, "Yes! I need to find my mom."

"Exactly, Vic," agreed Men-taur. "This is just the example for us to use. You became separated from your mother and you are keen to find her so that you can be a family again. That is a very powerful example, in fact. Love — what we are talking about here — can be one of the key emotions driving Passion. So, too, can hate, but let's stick with love. With understanding in his voice, Men-taur then queried, "Your love for your mother has not decreased since you were separated from her, right?"

"No, Sir," replied Vic with a look of pain stretching across his young face as he remembered how much he missed her.

"Will you stop looking for her?"

"No." Vic's answers were becoming increasingly quieter.

"What could keep you from looking for your mother?"

"Nothing," Vic replied somewhat weakly, as his head lowered and he thought about his lost, beloved mom.

"Are you sure, Vic?" pressed Men-taur.

"Yes," Vic replied quickly and indignantly, with a look of defiance in his eyes.

Then, beginning a cascade of quick questions, Men-taur pressed further. "So, you would face starvation in search of your mother?"

"Yes."

"You're willing to go without water to find your mother?"

"Yes!"

"You would step out from the protection of the Herd and step out on your own to find your mother?"

"YES!"

"And allow yourself to be exposed to the dangers of Lion and Leopard?"

"YES!" bellowed Vic angrily.

"Excellent, Vic!" finished Men-taur, purposefully lowering his tone so that Vic had to draw closer to hear him. "Your reactions to those questions, Vic, became more and more heated. Correct?"

"Yes," Vic warily agreed.

"Why?"

"Because you wouldn't let it go. It hurts to think about my mom, and you got me angry because the way you were asking was almost as if you were doubting my love for her," replied Vic with some residual irritation.

"Good, Vic. Good," reassured Men-taur, "Now, do you see, Vic, how you started out passionate about your mother and, by the end of those questions, your Passion had become intensely animated by both your love for your mother and — dare I say? — hatred and anger towards me and, perhaps, towards your own circumstances?"

"Yes," replied Vic meekly.

"Please understand, Vic, that in order to truly be passionate, you must first be able to harness both ends of the spectrum of your emotions in order to help you towards the outcome you desire in a controlled manner. In addition you should become adept at knowing and understanding what mix to use to fire your Passion, to give you energy and to help you succeed. This ability means that you can, with practice, switch on the energy you need to succeed in something which is, for you, a desire."

Men-taur casually looked around him and then back down at Vic. "When you are passionate about what you are doing or where you are heading," finished Men-taur, "it is easier to maintain the momentum; it then seems less like work."

At that point, a low rumble could be heard off in the distance. As they were slowly walking, both Vic and Men-taur began to feel the ground trembling. Vic furrowed his brow with a hint of uncertainty in his eyes, while Men-taur also frowned but with a look of recognition and wariness. Now, the other animals around them lifted their heads and pricked their ears; a few animals were starting to prance nervously. And then, breaking through a cluster of trees a few hundred yards away, came a mixed group of Beest and Zebra in stampede formation (which means to say there was no formation just momentum!) bellowing, snorting and kicking up clouds of thickening dust. Men-taur quickly assessed the stampede's direction and speed, and then dropped his shoulders and muzzle and quickly snorted, "Move!" as he shoved Vic with his shoulder in a direction on a tangent away from where the Beest were stampeding.

Without realizing it, Vic was being guided up a nearby knoll, which was partly ringed by a few dry acacia trees. Whilst Vic was looking ahead with widened eyes, pricked ears and a thumping heart, Men-taur was keeping both his eyes and his ears focused on the stampede, preparing himself to make any necessary adjustments.

Quickly, they reached the top and, when Vic turned to see what was happening, he noted that the group were cutting a widening swath through the Herd laid out before them, and more and more animals were swelling the numbers of the trampling marauders. Some animals managed to scatter themselves out of harm's way, while others did not; some of the unwary and unfocused came trampled and injured.

The trailing animals of the stampede thundered past and were submerged in a thick cloud of dust and panic a few hundred paces away. After a protracted watchful silence, Men-taur finally drew in a deep breath and exhaled slowly. He looked over the unsettled Herd, observing the damage and the disarray to determine his next course of action. And, after a few more moments, Men-taur turned from his far-reaching scan, looked down at Vic who seemed somewhat bewildered and then said, "That was a perfect example of Passion. I could not have given you a better immediate demonstration."

"Huh?" said Vic, utterly bewildered and questioning how Men-taur could merely take the scene before them as an 'example'. "What do you mean Men-taur?"

"Think about it, Vic. Passion is like that stampede: Once those Beest got started, it was hard for them to stop —or to even consider stopping. Passion, like a stampede, becomes infectious. Indeed, the

Passion gets passed on to every Beest involved who, in turn, passes it on to others. Those nearby catch it and become contagious with it, and the momentum ultimately grows for some time due to the vast and vibrant flow of energy and emotion which is being released. "In short, Vic, Passion must be contagious in order for you to be successful; you will need others around you to help fulfil your Vision and to create that School of Success, right?"

"Yes," replied Vic.

"Keep that in mind please, Vic," directed Men-taur before asking, "Now, Vic, what do you think was the cause of that stampede, that Passion?"

"I don't know... A Lion or some other danger," guessed Vic.

"Probably," answered Men-taur. "In all likelihood, that was probably the cause. You see, as Beest, we are understandably passionate about our safety. We aim to preserve our lives, and so we can become very passionate about being safe and fleeing from danger. Equally," Men-taur continued, "we can become passionate about our food and our water, as I am sure the other animals on the Journey do as well."

Men-taur took a moment to reflect on the scene before him and, no doubt, to allow Vic to absorb this concept. After watching the stampede dwindle, Men-taur turned back towards Vic. "You recall that my Vision is to lead the Herd for as many Journeys as I can while ensuring the best and safest routes where food and water are in abundant supply?"

Vic nodded and opened his mouth to speak, but something inside him told him to keep quiet as Men-taur took on a distant gaze, as if he were looking ahead and yet looking into his past. After a moment Men-taur then shared some of his experience.

"Well, this I have done successfully over the past four Journeys. As such, my experience has enabled me to determine the best route each Journey, with each Journey following a similar but not exactly the same path each time." Men-taur paused for a moment before continuing. "Do you think, Vic, that my way — the way in which I have chosen to guide the Herd through the Journey has been the right way?" Men-taur looked down at Vic but Vic sensed the question was rhetorical and so remained silent. "Of course, I believe my way has been appropriate and well considered, but everyone differs. You see, a few other Herd leaders have, over the Journeys, tried to persuade me that there is a better route. And, as you may have noticed, some of our numbers here are reducing as the amalgamated Herd now diverges; this is because these other leaders are leading their Herds along a different and wider path towards the setting sun, as I understand it. As yet, I have not been persuaded to adopt their route, which is supposedly better; instead, I continue on this chosen path as I am personally convinced that my way is the best way, and so I am sticking to it as it allows me to fulfil my Vision. And, although every creature is entitled to their own opinion and Vision, I will nevertheless passionately argue that this route is the best one to take if anyone tries to convince me into thinking otherwise."

Vic nodded and immediately admired Men-taur's sense of determination.

"Also, please note, Vic, that I accept that other routes may, in fact, be good and, quite possibly, they may even be better. If you were to ask them the same question, it is also quite possible that they would even concede the same. And there lies one aspect of Passion of which you need to be aware: Sometimes, Passion can blind you to other possibilities and opportunities which may ultimately be better than those you have chosen to allow you to reach your Vision."

"From where I stand, Vic, Passion is like sunshine." Men-taur compared. "Take a look at this Bee, Vic." Men-taur pointed with his right fore-hoof towards a small patch of grass clinging to the dry soil where a drone was busily rubbing its front feet over its antennae.

Sometimes, Passion can blind you to other possibilities and opportunities which may ultimately be better than those you have chosen to allow you to reach your Vision.

Once Vic had sidled up to where he could see where exactly Men-taur was pointing, Men-taur continued his comparison.

"The Bee uses the sun to guide its way to and from its hive to various sources of food. That same sun also helps to keep that Bee warm and to ultimately continue on its daily Journey. That Bee knows that the sun will always be there, and it uses the sun to help it to fulfil its Journey and its Vision. Passion does the exact same thing, Vic; it provides us with energy and warmth, and subsequently helps guide us on our Journey to our Vision."

Vic nodded in understanding.

"Now, here's another question for you, Vic: Will that Bee ever stop looking for food and fulfilling its role in the hive, Vic?"

"No."

"Why not?"

"Because it knows what its role is," stated Vic, although somewhat uncertainly.

"Yes, that's true," Men-taur agreed. "And also, because it knows its role and how it fits into the Vision of the hive, it pursues its role with Passion. This Bee will keep fulfilling its role until its life on its Journey has ended."

Passion is like sunshine: It provides us with energy and warmth, and subsequently helps guide us on our Journey to our Vision.

Men-taur finished speaking but continued onwards. His head was, once again, scanning the land and the Herd before and around him.

By now, the sun was hovering, suspended just above the Horizon, lengthening the shadows of all that obstructed its light. Time had passed quickly. Men-taur suddenly stopped, flared his nostrils as he inhaled deeply and concluded, "Vic, it is time to conclude your lesson on this second success factor — Passion and being passionate about your Vision. So, as with the last lesson, please summarize the key points on Passion. Note, too, Vic, that in order to help you further grasp, understand and apply this and your further lessons, please link these lessons back to your Vision, okay?"

"Okay," Vic agreed.

Taking a moment to order his thoughts, Vic then recounted his understanding of what he had learned.

"The first key point actually relates to my Vision. When I speak about my Vision with Passion, it gains power and energizes me. Secondly, in order for me to be successful, my Passion must be an all-consuming desire for my Vision and for what I am doing at the time in order to see my Vision achieved." Noting Men-taur's cocked eyebrow and, almost imperceptible nod of understanding and encouragement, Vic continued. "Thirdly, it is best for me to use — in a controlled manner — a spectrum of strong emotions in the right mix to bolster my Passion, energize me, and to therefore help me to progress towards my Vision. And when I become experienced with this I will be able to switch on and off the right mix of emotions that will fuel my Passion."

Men-taur nodded enthusiastically.

"The fourth point is that my Passion must be contagious if I am to succeed and achieve my Vision. I need to become infectious with my Passion because I need others who become Passionate about my Vision to see it reached." Vic paused for a moment before continuing. "You gave me one caution though, Men-taur," Vic stressed. "Sometimes, Passion may blind me to other possibilities and opportunities that may be better than the ones I have chosen to achieve my Vision; this is something which I will always need to bear in mind. And, finally," concluded Vic, "Passion is like sunshine; it will give me energy and warmth and help to guide me towards my Vision."

Men-taur smiled with appreciation. "Once again, Vic, you have summarized very well. Well done."

"So, as I always do upon concluding any meeting, until we next meet, I recommend you carefully consider these key points and what they mean to you — specifically in relation to you achieving your own Vision. This will help you to clarify both your Vision and to also heighten your Passion. Once again, when you do this, you will also begin to experience a greater awareness of the Rhythm, particularly as it relates to you and the path before you."

Men-taur turned away momentarily and then back to Vic.
"Now, I must be off to see about ensuring that all is prepared for the
Herd tonight," shared Men-taur. As he was about to head off ahead, he
added, "Be prepared to share any insights and progress you have made
the next time we meet. I'll keep an eye out for any other Herds where
your mother might be. And I'll also let you know when the next lesson
will be initiated." With that, Men-taur trotted off with puffs of dust
from his hooves punctuating his steps.

As before, Vic now felt a mixture of excitement about his future
and emptiness that Men-taur had gone. However, his contemplation
was short-lived because he then realized the emptiness was further
accentuated because his stomachs were now grumbling audibly.
He was also thirsty. And so, Vic allowed his primeval urges to kick in
and set out in search for food and water before nightfall.

"A great leader's courage to fulfil his vision
comes from passion, not position."

John C Maxwell

"The key that unlocks energy is desire.
It's also the key to a long and interesting life.
If we expect to create any drive, any real force within
ourselves, we have to get excited."

Earl Nightingale

Exercise 2 - **Your Passion**

As with the previous exercise, please consider this exercise carefully and thoughtfully, as it pertains to successfully achieving your Vision that you noted previously.

1. On a scale of 1-10*, how strong is your level of Passion for the Vision you wrote down for Exercise 1? _____

2. In the event that you scored yourself below an 8, what 3 things do you need to be and/or do which will help to increase your Passion for your Vision to an 8+?

_____

_____

_____

_____

_____

_____

_____

_____

_____

_____

_____

_____

_____

_____

_____

* For this and the other exercises, please note that a score of 1 represents the weakest and a score of 10 represents the strongest.

Chapter Six

"The will must be stronger than the skill."

Muhammad Ali

"Our greatest weakness lies in giving up.
The most certain way to succeed is always
to try just one more time."

Thomas Edison

The following few weeks blurred together for Vic. As before, he caught glimpses of Men-taur and, occasionally, Men-taur dropped by to briefly check on Vic — but it was always brief; Men-taur did, after all, have a Herd to lead.

Each day passed similarly to the one before, and the expectation of what lay ahead seemed to always be constant. From sun-up to sun-down, the Herd kept moving, always seeking to slake its thirst and satisfy its hunger. At this time of year, it seemed as if the quest for these needs got longer, hotter and dustier.

Each evening, it was a time to let the exhaustion rush in and win over an uneasy sleep. Night brought with it its own tension, which differed from the tension of the day; predators found it a favorite time to strike. Several times each night, Vic had been awoken to the alarm of another predator raid. Such raids brought confusion and compounded the exhaustion due to the further stress and anxiety from the ensuing stampede. And it brought back the floods of memories of events which had ultimately led to Vic's present situation.

During the raids Vic had to be particularly careful; he was, after all, still small and an orphan. He had to have his wits about him. On several occasions, he had narrowly missed getting kicked and trampled on. Once, he had just managed to avoid running right over the edge of a rocky outcropping. A few other Beest were not so lucky; because of the height of the fall, those Beest became injured and, ultimately, became the targeted prey for the predators — the Lion and Hyena which were harrying the Herd.

However, occasionally, ripples of hope passed through the Herd when, in the distance, dark clouds gathered and accompanying thunder rumbled lowly, promising rain ahead. And rain meant water and new grass. Such hope helped urge each animal on despite the fear and the coinciding frightful events.

However, some animals — Beest and other plain game alike — seemed to be fading despite the forever-burning hope. The Journey was taking its toll. After weeks of hardship, some of the old Beest and the young calves alike became too weak to continue; it was difficult for any of the Herd to watch them drop away or just collapse — and it was even harder to leave them behind.

The ones which died from old age or even exhaustion were fortunate. On the other hand, it was difficult for Vic — and no doubt for the rest of the Herd — to listen to the panicked cries and struggles of those fallen upon by the predators. The weak and the exhausted were easy meals for Lion, Leopard and Hyena — and the predators got plenty of free meals.

Each day along the way, there was evidence of this scenario; clusters of frenzied Vultures could be seen swarming over the remains of some unfortunate animal which had lost its way along the Journey.

Vic reflected on the sacrifice of these animals. He was ashamed. He was grateful. Their death meant that the Herd, himself included, could pass by a little less harried. As the Journey progressed, it meant that this would likely occur more and more and safeguard the rest of the Herd with a safe passage and slow down the predators behind them. It did not bear thinking about that there were predators ahead of them too.

Each day, to keep his spirits up, Vic would reflect on his Vision. At times, he would speak it out with Passion. At such outbursts, the other Beest around him would look at him with concern wondering, perhaps, whether the sun was affecting him. For a time, those same Beest would give him a wide berth.

Each outburst seemed to get stronger. Each outburst increased Vic's clarity of his Vision. Each outburst added fuel to his Passion.

On the tail of his latest outburst, Vic was startled when he heard just behind him, "Impressive. I can see and hear you have taken our lessons to heart."

Vic turned with widened eyes to see Men-taur almost now alongside. Inwardly calming his racing heart, Vic blurted out a less-than-controlled, "Men-taur! You startled me!"

With a smile in his eyes, Men-taur chuckled, "It is always worthwhile keeping my students on their toes." After a brief pause, Men-taur continued, "I'll give you a moment to calm down. Take a deep breath. Actually, take three slow, deep breaths."

Vic complied.

"Yes, that's good. And another."

Vic did as requested once again.

"Good. You okay now, Vic?"

"Yes. Thank you."

"Excellent. Today is a good day to continue your lessons," stated Men-taur. "Are you ready for your third lesson, Vic?"

"Yes, Sir!" Vic replied enthusiastically.

Vic had initially been wondering if this was going to be another of those quick visits, but clearly not. He had been getting frustrated that his lessons had stalled, but now he could feel himself getting excited about learning what the next lesson would involve.

Without waiting Men-taur began, "Good. Now, as before, I would like you to summarize what you have learned so far from the first two lessons."

Men-taur's presence and expectant silence encouraged Vic. As they walked side-by-side, Vic started, "My Vision is what will drive me forward for Journeys to come and my Passion will fuel me to achieve my Vision. By combining the right emotions I can strengthen my Passion and make it infectious so that, when combined with my Vision, other Beest will hopefully catch hold and follow me."

"Good. And..." Men-taur encouraged.

"And I must be aware that my Passion may sometimes blind me to other options and opportunities as I Journey toward my Vision," finished Vic.

"That's good, Vic. Tell me, how often are you meant to review your Vision? How are you to look at your Horizon?" queried Men-taur.

My Vision is what will drive me forward for Journeys to come and my Passion will fuel me to achieve my Vision.

"You suggested that I am to meditate on my Vision in the morning and the evening of each day; this is what I have been doing," Vic answered, trying to impress Men-taur.

Men-taur nodded and added simply, "And what has been the result of that?"

Hurriedly, Vic replied, "My Vision has become clearer each time."

That seemed to satisfy Men-taur. Vic breathed a sigh of relief. Before he could complete his sigh, Men-taur asked, "And what about your Horizon?"

Berating himself inwardly, Vic answered, "Each day my experience grows, and so I must always take the time to view it for any changes which have the potential to impact me and my Vision."

"Okay. That's good," agreed Men-taur. "Now can I ask, what will keep you from achieving your Vision? What could get in the way of your Vision?"

With the innocence of youth, Vic mistakenly replied, "Nothing."

"Really?" questioned Men-taur.

Just the tone of Men-taur's reply made Vic wince.

Before Vic could dig a hole for himself with perhaps another thoughtless or innocent reply, Men-taur opened up, "Well, Vic. This is a good time then to get on with your third lesson. Today's lesson complements the first two success factors, which will each help you to harness the Rhythm within and to ultimately achieve your full potential. Today's lesson is about Commitment," stated Men-taur.

As Men-taur finished speaking, a ripple of excitement washed over them from the Herd ahead. Distracted, Vic stopped to ponder what this meant. Men-taur tapped his right fore-hoof to regain Vic's attention. "Vic, back to your lesson!"

"Oh, sorry!" apologized Vic. "But what's all the excitement about, Men-taur?" Vic asked.

"You'll find out soon enough," assured Men-taur. "Let's veer over there and get atop that rocky outcrop so that we can see what is going on ahead," directed Men-taur as he began to lead in that direction.

Lesson 3 - Commitment

Vic followed in Men-taur's wake as they cut across the general direction of the movement of the Herd. Vic felt the heat beating down on his back as the sun reached its zenith. He choked on the swirling dust as they moved. Despite choking, Vic kept on Men-taur's leeward side to keep from being buffeted by other animals. Men-taur paid little heed to such a concern as the Herd around them always gave way to their leader; a perk of leadership, Vic thought. Vic also noted that Men-taur nodded and acknowledged most of the Beest as they passed, and even a few of the antelope. Vic realized that courtesy and manners were very important to Men-taur and to leadership — as they should be with all of the animals.

After a few minutes and a bit of effort (at least for Vic), the two animals mounted the outcrop. From this vantage point they were able to see the Herd and the accompanying plains. Vic noted that there seemed to be more and more animals funneling into the area. In fact, up ahead, through the settling dust, he thought he could make out that the Herd seemed to have stopped or, rather, was milling about where there appeared to be a gap in the land that fell away on their right.

...courtesy and manners were
very important ... to leadership.

Vic turned to ask Men-taur what all this meant. But, before he could, Men-taur moved such that Vic could see past him and, with that view, Vic sharply caught his breath.

There, before Vic, was an incredible sight. "What is that?" he asked.

"That, Vic, is the River. And that is what every animal here must cross to continue the Journey to the richer plains ahead," answered Men-taur.

Only then did it register with Vic that his ears had been hearing an increasing rumbling sound. He had attributed it to some thunder or a stampede in the distance. Now, he realized, what he had been hearing was the surging River.

Vic stood there with his mouth gaping as he took in the beautiful view. Parallel to where they stood, a muddied River was churning and boiling over some boulders. The roar of the River told of its power. Upstream there had clearly been some heavy rains typical of this time of year; these rains had fed the previously dry riverbed and now it was advancing wildly in flood. With that thought, Vic turned to Men-taur who was looking at him with detached interest.

"Now is a perfect time to start your lesson," declared Men-taur.

"But what about the River?" asked a still stunned Vic.

"What about it? The River is key to explaining today's lesson. To cross the River means you will need Commitment," emphasized Men-taur.

A feeling of dread began to well up inside Vic. He asked himself how he was going to cross and, in a split second, Vic began to panic internally —he didn't like the prospect of having to cross one little bit.

"Vic... Vic!" Men-taur snapped loudly.

Vic snapped out of his introspection. His legs were trembling. His eyes were wide. His nostrils flared as his breaths came in short and sharp bursts.

"Vic, everything will be okay. Listen to me," Men-taur urged reassuringly.

Only barely holding himself together with his pride, Vic responded, "Yes, Men-taur."

Vic found that he had to concentrate on Men-taur's face or he would get sucked back into staring at the River, and would soon become engulfed in the fear of crossing that which was clearly so powerful, strong — and dangerous.

Men-taur quickly maneuvered himself to block Vic's view of the River; thankfully, the outcropping was quite large, and so he guided Vic away from the outcropping's edge. When he was sure that Vic could at least not see any suggestion of the River, he resumed. "Vic, do you remember we were discussing what could potentially keep you from achieving your Vision? You replied that there was nothing. Do you remember?" Men-taur looked at Vic and continued, "Based on your reaction to the River, maybe you would like to give me an answer to that question again?"

Vic stood there in silence for a brief moment; now that he had something to think about other than the River, his thoughts slowed and he attended to answering the question, realizing how his first answer had been so naïve and thoughtless. "The River could keep me from my Vision."

"How?" asked Men-taur simply.

"Well, if I do not cross it, my Vision is in jeopardy."

"That's right. The River represents an obstacle — in this case, a significant one. It could very well be the first big obstacle in the way of achieving your Vision but it is highly likely it will not be the last one either," stressed Men-taur. "Obstacles, you see, can be as big or as small as you make them; all obstacles can either be perceived as a blockage to your Vision or they can be seen as an exercise to helping you achieve it, to helping you deserve it. What you must understand is that obstacles make you stronger when you are able to view them as exercise. As such, when considering your Vision, Vic, you must also consider what obstacles may arise that could potentially hinder your progress; by anticipating them, you can plan for them and will subsequently be better equipped to either avoid them altogether or more easily overcome them."

Vic nodded in understanding, listening intently. He realized that, based on his reaction to seeing the River, he needed to grasp the importance and content of this lesson. He felt and knew deep down within him that it was critical for both his life and his Vision. At this moment, Vic also realized how fortunate he was to be learning this lesson one-to-one. He wondered how the other Beest and animals managed to face crossing the River without the benefit of a teacher like Men-taur.

Obstacles make you stronger when you are able to view them as exercise.

Vic cleared his thoughts as he realized Men-taur had resumed and seemed to be answering his thoughts.

"...Take the River, for example. I know that, as part of my Vision, I have to lead as many Journeys of the Herd as safely and securely as I can, but I cannot avoid the River. I can, however, determine when, where and, to a certain extent, how to cross. Also, I make a point of training up some key members across the Herd who I assign to be part of the Crossing Committee; together, we review our past experience of these crossings and establish how we can improve our success of getting as many of the Herd across safely. From there, we are able to establish a Crossing Plan. Once that is agreed upon, each respective member will speak with their respective groups to ensure that every Beest is duly prepared for the Crossing."

Vic listened keenly, mesmerized by Men-taur and his ability to forward plan, and how less daunting it made the prospect of crossing any obstacle seem.

"The key lesson we aim for every Beest to learn prior to the Crossing is that Commitment will get you to the other side — without absolute Commitment, there is often only failure awaiting."

Vic caught the emphasis of Men-taur's last point and asked, "What happens if one fails?"

Men-taur replied, "Well, Vic, that is a question of which I am sure you know the answer. In the case of crossing the River, failure usually means death — death by drowning or starvation because the food is scarce this side of the River. There is also the chance of a Beest being trampled or killed by Crocodiles or other predators."

Without absolute commitment, there is often
only failure awaiting.

"Should you fail during other parts of the Journey, well, unlike the Crossing, there is less chance of death and more the chance to learn something. All failures are an opportunity to learn something; each failure is a lesson and so, in essence, nothing is ever really a complete failure — you just need to ensure that you apply that learning in order to avoid repetition of the same mistake — a mistake that could ultimately cost your life. Understood?"

"Yes, Men-taur."

"Good. Now let's get down from here and move ahead to the crossing point."

Vic followed closely while struggling with the thoughts that threatened to swamp him: He had never done a Crossing before and he was fighting with thoughts of doubt. He felt he needed to tell Men-taur.

All failures are an opportunity to learn something;
each failure is a lesson.

"Men-taur?" Vic asked.

"Yes," came Men-taur's brief reply.

"I am having some doubts about being able to make the Crossing. I have never done one before and I don't know how," admitted Vic.

"Vic, that does not surprise me. I, too, had doubts the first time I made the Crossing," Men-taur answered.

"You?" remarked Vic incredulously.

"Yes. Anytime we try something new, it is not unexpected that there will be doubts. Take the first time you got to your feet and took your first steps after you were born — did you have doubts then?" asked Men-taur.

"Yes," replied Vic.

"But who was there by your side?"

"My mom."

"Exactly. And with her encouragement did your doubts go away?"

"Yes."

"Well, this situation is no different. Well, actually it is — this time you will have far more encouragement from all of those around you," added Men-taur. "After all, you will not be alone for your Crossing." Men-taur gave the notion time to sink in before asking, "So, how do you feel now, Vic?"

"Better, thank you."

"Right, now let's get to the head of the queue," declared Men-taur. And, with that, they wound their way through the crowds. It took them time to press through the Herd. The occasional Beest ahead of them became irritated when asked to move aside. But, as soon as they saw it was Men-taur requesting a path through, they gave way with a grunt or apology. Vic heard Men-taur reassure these and other Beest as they passed with a casual, "Good day for the Crossing!" or "Remember what's on the other side — food!" The general response was a nod and a smile. Occasionally, one or two would laugh.

Men-taur leaned over to whisper to Vic, "The Herd is always tense just before the Crossing. Now is a critical time to encourage others."

And, with that, they continued, only this time, to Men-taur's amusement and approval, Vic added his own version of encouragement to Men-taur's, "Nothing like a good Crossing to work up an appetite!"

Shortly, there was no one before them — they had made their way to the front. Just off to the side of the breach that led down the bank to the surging River was a small raised patch of flat stone.

"Wait here," Men-taur said as he stepped up onto the stone.

Vic had to crane his head and neck to see Men-taur, who had now turned to face the Herd. Apart from the background roar of the River, a silence descended amongst the Herd, with only the sound of breathing from the compressed bodies of numerous Beest.
All seemed to be waiting.

Men-taur inhaled deeply to fill his lungs. "FELLOW BEEST, THE TIME HAS COME FOR ANOTHER CROSSING," boomed Men-taur. "THIS TIME IT LOOKS LIKE WE ARE BLESSED; THE RIVER IS NOT NEARLY AS FULL AS IT HAS BEEN IN THE PAST. THAT CAN ONLY MEAN THAT THIS TIME WILL BE EASIER. THIS TIME MORE OF US WILL MAKE IT TO THE OTHER SIDE. THIS TIME WE WILL HAVE AN EVEN BIGGER CELEBRATION! YOU ALL SHOULD HAVE BEEN BRIEFED ON THE CROSSING. FOR THOSE OF YOU WHO HAVE NOT, PLEASE SPEAK WITH YOUR GROUP LEADER. PLEASE AWAIT THE SIGNAL TO BEGIN THE CROSSING. FOCUS ON THE OTHER SIDE. REMEMBER TO KEEP MOVING FORWARD. REMEMBER THE GOLDEN RULE — *HOOF IT!* GOOD DAY AND GOOD CROSSING!"

A brief hush followed. No cheers echoed through the Herd as Vic had expected. Vic realized this was no time for excitement; every Beest knew the Crossing was imperative to their survival. The Crossing was a serious matter; the cheers would come later — but only from those who had not lost a friend or family member to the roaring waters.

Gradually, the general murmuring and snorting returned. Vic noted that the tone had changed; it was now less random and more focused on what lay ahead, and apparent anticipation was present in the air. Vic caught snippets of comments and conversations from nearby.

"I just want to get this over with."

"Looks easy this time. Remember the Crossing two Journeys ago? That was a doozy."

"Now, stick by my side, Dear. We don't want to get separated. Remember to keep your eyes on me and the opposite bank."

"What are they waiting for?"

"Remember the golden rule — *Hoof it!*"

Then, every conversation just blurred as Men-taur beckoned Vic with a nod to his side.

Once at Men-taur's side, Vic could see the concentration of Beest; never before had he witnessed so many together, nor so tightly packed. A nervous tension fluttered through the air.

"Over the Journeys," Men-taur began, "this has proven to be the best Crossing point. The bank is less steep here on both sides. Also, the River has just come around a sharp corner, and so some of its momentum has been broken and lost, making it easier for us to cross."

"When will we cross Men-taur?" asked Vic.

"Soon," replied Men-taur.

"I need to supervise the start from here. Each time, despite our best efforts to urge control, a frenzy to cross breaks out and, with that, comes danger. It's that danger which can then lead to panic, especially when the Crocodiles show up and when a few Beest, regrettably the old, the lame and the young, get stuck in the mud and then trampled or fall prey to the River lurkers. In the panic, some calves get separated from their mothers. I have even seen some of them cross two or three times looking for each other."

"How can we stop this from happening?" asked Vic.

"We can't really, Vic. It's unfortunate and sad but it is often the Way of Things. We have tried but, so far, we have not found a solution. In some respect, it is Nature's way of weeding out the weak from the strong — and it is the strong, physically and mentally, that we need in our Herd."

"Both after and prior to each Crossing, I gather the group leaders to review what has happened previously and, as best we can, we consider what we can expect for the next Crossing. We discuss how we can improve future Crossings to ensure more Beest get across and less die. From there we are able to make a plan which we believe will achieve our outcome — to lead as many Beest across safely."

"Just remember Vic that the Journey is part of the Circle of Life, and this is one of those times which is ultimately down to the Way of Things. At this part of the Journey, we are driven forward both by what lays ahead — the promise of fresh and lush grassland — and also by the opposite promise of starvation or worse for those who choose to stay on this side or who otherwise fail to cross," responded Men-taur.

Vic still did not fully understand. His puzzled look prompted Men-taur to continue.

"Getting back to your lesson, Vic, this is a great example of Commitment to what lies ahead. Without absolute Commitment it is very unlikely a Beest will make it to the other side. But, with absolute Commitment, the odds are in your favor. This is not a time for doubt — it's a time for resolve."

Pausing briefly to ensure that Vic was listening, Men-taur emphasized, "Vic, this is a real life and death situation. There is no going back. There is only going forward. That's where your Vision lies. This is truly a survival of the fittest, for only the fittest will help the Herd to continue on for many Journeys into our future."

Just then, there was a loud bellow from a bull standing on the side opposite side of the gap that descended to the River. With that, there was a hush and, without any apparent signal, the Beest surged forward to the lip of the embankment and then stopped.

"We'll continue in a moment," whispered Men-taur, "For now, watch."

The bull then leaped down from where he was and landed on the bank ahead of the front line of Beest. He didn't stop. Bellowing, he charged right into the surging water. For a moment, he seemed to stop as the water suspended his progress, and then he half-lunged and half-leaped until he was swimming with his head pointed towards the opposite bank.

Vic noticed that there was a hush all round as every eye watched the bull's efforts.

After what seemed ages, Vic noted a change in the rhythm of the bull's movement. And then, with his eyes straining, Vic could just see from his vantage point that the bull was again lunging in the water. And then...

"He made it!" Vic exclaimed with his heart in his throat.

At the same time, a bellow reached them from the opposite bank. Immediately, a chorus of matching bellows answered the call. Then, like a brown and gray avalanche, the first wave of Beest teamed down the bank and hit the water, spurred on by the success of the first brave Beest to tackle the obstacle dividing life and death.

The Crossing had begun!

Vic stood by Men-taur as they watched a stream of bodies flow down the bank. As Men-taur had forewarned, some Beest, including a few calves got stuck in the mud. They weren't stuck for long. They got trampled. Their cries were agonizing to hear. Vic looked up at Men-taur who had a saddened and resigned look on his face.

"Vic, look." Men-taur indicated with his horns to the opposite bank. The first Beest were now struggling onto the firm land.

The distraction helped. Vic felt hope return to him. "I can do it!" Vic said to himself.

"Of course you can do it. I'll be right by your side," Men-taur assured.

And, with that, Men-taur motioned that it was time for them to join the Herd and take their place ready for the Crossing.

"Let's quickly finish your lesson for it is time for us to cross," Men-taur urged. "Vic, you must complete this Crossing to achieve your Vision. Do you understand?"

"Yes, Men-taur."

"This Crossing is a stepping stone towards your Vision, Vic. Each milestone is important. Your Commitment is bolstered each time you achieve such a stepping stone. Along the way to your Vision, there will be many milestones. It is, therefore, important that, when thinking of your Vision each day, you consider and set what will be the milestones leading back from then until now and from now until then. You must remain committed to the course you have chosen towards your Vision, Vic; this means that you must be committed to the next goal or milestone. And, each time you achieve a milestone, your Commitment will increase," stressed Men-taur. "So, Vic, what is your first milestone?"

"To cross the River safely," Vic replied simply and surely.

"Excellent, Vic," Men-taur said encouragingly, "The way you worded that was very clear. Some Beest might say their aim was to cross the River. That would fall short and so, likely, would they. Now, this Crossing is a significant milestone for you. One of the secrets to a successful Crossing is to know your outcome. Know how you are going to achieve it, create a plan, believe in it and stick to it," Men-taur asserted.

Each time you achieve a milestone,
your Commitment will increase.

"So, Vic, what's your outcome and what's your plan?"

After a moment to get his thoughts right, Vic answered, "Having seen the others now make the Crossing, my outcome is to reach the other side safely and confidently with you by my side. I will achieve it by focusing on the opposite bank across the River, knowing that I am making progress towards my Vision; remembering the golden rule, I will *"Hoof it!"*"

"Excellent, Vic. Simple and sure," Men-taur responded approvingly.

...know your outcome.

"Just before we head down the bank, as a helpful tip to help you to get a clear picture of your Vision in mind, stir in your Passion from your heart and make your Commitment to reach the other side. Do that now and you will make it to the other side," assured Men-taur.

"Those of us who have done this before know that Vision plus Passion plus Commitment is a crucial mix which, when applied consistently with each Crossing, will result in success. Without that powerful combination, it is probable that you would be met with failure."

"And, finally," finished Men-taur, "when it comes to achieving your goals, it is worth remembering that achieving them is like swimming: When you are really serious about getting to the other side, you've got to take what's in front of you and keep pushing it behind you. You must remember — you are either consistent or you are non-existent," finished Men-taur.

...you are either consistent or
you are non-existent...

Vic took it all in; he knew this would be a critical moment in his brief life; he knew he had to cross the River; he knew that Men-taur would be by his side; he knew he must succeed. And, with that, he stepped into the mass of Beest channeling through the gap.

Men-taur turned his head and stared searchingly into Vic's eyes. "Are you ready for this, Vic?"

"Ready as I'll ever be," Vic responded with only a hint of trepidation.

Men-taur nodded before letting out a bellow as they both teetered on the lip of the embankment before being carried down it with the momentum and force of other Beest behind, before and alongside.

Vic's heart was pounding and his feet skidded, slipped, and churned beneath him. Already, he was gasping for air from the press of bodies — and then he hit the water. His feet were swept out from under him and he quickly became disoriented.

Fortunately, Men-taur was on his downstream side, and so he was only forced into Men-taur's side. "Come on, Vic, 'Hoof it!'" Men-taur snorted encouragingly.

Men-taur's words brought Vic back to the moment, and he began to churn through the water. Quickly, two things happened: First, he began to move ahead with Men-taur, and second, his hooves lost touch with the river-bottom.

He was swimming.

Vic had a flashback to the time he crossed the watering hole and met Men-taur for the very first time. This time, however, was completely different — different because, this time, the water was moving and moving fast. But, despite the difference in depth, despite the surging rapids and the panic amongst the Beest, Vic realized he had done this before and, even back then, he had set a target and focused on his goal with both Passion and Commitment. Then he had been a success and so, in Vic's logic, he would be a success now.

All of this happened in the briefest of moments. Vic snapped back to the present by Men-taur's snorts and by the water filling his own nostrils. Vic blew hard and then added some extra power to his thrusting hind legs to help his muzzle become clear of the water. Other surging bodies pressed him from every angle, but Men-taur's strong and confident presence and occasional snort of encouragement kept Vic focused on the bank ahead.

After what seemed an entire day from sun-up to sun-down, Vic was finally able to see the pattern of some of swimming Beest ahead change to lunging up the riverbank. That view spurred Vic on and, shortly after, Vic found his legs touching the bottom again.

He had made it!

Vic struggled out of the water and realized his legs were trembling. He felt exhausted. And, despite having been in a cold River, Vic could feel that he was actually sweating.

"Come on, Vic," urged Men-taur as he headed up the steep bank, "keep moving forward until we are clear of the bank. We can then watch the others cross and finish your lesson."

Vic could muster only a grunt in reply as tiredness swept over his body and mind. Panting with the continued effort, Vic's legs tremored their way up the bank. He followed doggedly after Men-taur.

Once over the brow of the bank, Men-taur turned sharply to get out of the flow of Beest. Within a few paces, they found themselves once again alone. The two Beest turned and watched as a collection of cows, bulls, adolescents and calves moved past; some even had the gumption to kick up their heels in celebration and excitement.

All Vic could think about was how tired he felt.

"Well done, Vic! Well done!" said Men-taur with an enthusiastic shake of his horns.

"Thank you," Vic panted. "I didn't realize I would be so exhausted."

Men-taur looked at his young charge. "Ah, yes. Success does not come without expending some effort. In this case, a lot of it." Men-taur gave a smile of satisfaction and pride. "So, aside from feeling exhausted, how do you feel now that you have completed your first Crossing?" Men-taur asked, stressing the last three words.

"I'm not sure I can put it into words," replied Vic.

"That's understandable. You might not feel the full impact of this significant achievement until later tonight or tomorrow once you have had time to reflect," shared Men-taur. "But, you have overcome your first major obstacle and that is quite a remarkable thing for any Beest. I'll give you a few more moments to collect your thoughts and your breath before we finish today's lesson. So, you focus on breathing."

It took a bit of time for Vic to feel that he was able to carry on with a conversation. Men-taur, meanwhile, stood watching out over the Herd as they crossed and passed by.

When Men-taur thought Vic had recovered sufficiently, he resumed the lesson. "Today's lesson has been all about Commitment and how it is a critical factor in being a success at anything you undertake and, most importantly, in achieving your Vision. As with the last lesson, Vic, please recap the key points and tie them up with what you have learned so far."

Vic quickly reviewed all that happened and, as best he could, all that Men-taur had shared about Commitment before beginning. "We started on how any obstacle to my Vision can actually be seen as an exercise to strengthen me on my way towards it. Secondly, it is best for me to anticipate and plan exactly how to manage such obstacles; if I am not committed, I will likely fail. And, linking to the second is the third point, that each failure — mine or that of others — is an opportunity for me to learn. Fourthly, in order to successfully achieve my Vision, I must keep moving forward; I must – 'Hoof it!'"

As before, Men-taur stood watching Vic summarize, adding a nod or a grin each time Vic hit the mark.

"The next point was that only with absolute Commitment are the odds in my favor to achieving my Vision. Along the way I must establish milestones so that each time I achieve one, my Commitment will increase. And, finally," concluded Vic, "by knowing my outcome and combining my Passion and Commitment, I will be more likely to achieve it; however, I must be consistent in my approach."

"Excellent, Vic. You have captured the core of this lesson superbly. Now, it is time for me to head off as I need to meet with the group heads to review how the Crossing went. Please reflect on what you have accomplished today and on what you have learned about Commitment, specifically how it relates to you achieving your own Vision. I know that after today you will begin to feel the Rhythm more strongly regarding your path; I know because it did for me when I completed my first Crossing." Men-taur gave Vic a smile which said he was proud and Vic had done well.

"I look forward to continuing these lessons, Vic. Well done again for today. As before, be prepared to share what new insights you have gained from this and the other lessons." Men-taur then smiled approvingly and simply said, "I'll see you in a while."

Vic watched Men-taur drift away into the Herd as with the end of the previous lessons. And, as before, Vic felt a pang of loneliness now that Men-taur had gone. But, this time, there was the unmistakable additional feeling — one of Commitment.

"In the realm of commitment, all that is available is possibilities and solutions."

Unknown

"When you get into a tight place and everything goes against you, never give up then, for that is just the time that the tide will turn."

Harriet Beecher Stowe

Exercise 3 - **Your Commitment**

As with the previous exercises, please consider this exercise carefully and thoughtfully, as it pertains to successfully achieving your Vision that you noted previously.

1.   On a scale of 1-10*, how strong is your level of Commitment for the Vision you wrote down for Exercise 1? _____

2.   In the event that you scored yourself below an 8, what 3 things do you need to be and/or do which will help to increase your Commitment for your Vision to an 8+?

_____

_____

_____

_____

_____

_____

_____

_____

_____

_____

_____

_____

_____

_____

* For this and the other exercises, please note that a score of 1 represents the weakest and a score of 10 represents the strongest.

Chapter Seven

"The one unchangeable certainty is that nothing is certain or unchangeable."

John F Kennedy

"There are two primary choices in life; to accept conditions as they exist or accept the responsibility for changing them."

Denis Waitley

The Crossing had taken most of the day, and by the time the Herd had crossed, the sun was low on the Horizon. And, while some Beest just wanted to put the River behind them, some, like Vic, returned to it.

Regrettably, scattered along the River's edge in various places, were Beest who had not made it; despite the lateness of the day, the vultures were descending. Vic reflected that, clearly, there would always be victims along the Journey. And he realized that loss was just part of the Way of Things.

Vic was brought out of his reflection by the sound of some cows searching in anguish for their lost calves. Vic could sense their despair. He watched the painful spectacle as if drawn to it. Occasionally, a bawling and frightened calf would be reunited with its mother after having been separated during the Crossing. The joy of these reunions often moved Vic to tears as he recalled his own separation. Despite the joy of seeing mother and calf nuzzle each other and head away, Vic felt in his own heart the reawakened ache of losing his mother, and how she must have called for him without success.

Vic had actually returned to the River to reflect on what he had achieved and what he had learned about Commitment and its part in his Journey. After taking a wary drink at the River's edge, Vic turned his back and headed up the bank to return to the fold of the Herd with the one predominant thought echoing in his mind, *"Hoof it!"*

Despite his fatigue, Vic still had to walk a fair distance to reach where the Herd was settling into their groups for the night. It was as though the unwritten rule was to put as much distance between the River and the Herd as a way of putting the hardship of it behind them. This made sense to Vic; the Crossing was not something he wanted to go through every day, and now that it was behind him, he would be able to focus on what he had learned and begin to apply his learnings in the days ahead.

The moon now proved the stronger light in the sky as the day transitioned into night. Stars began to dance and flicker across the heavenly canopy. Snores began to rumble across the air as more animals succumbed to the exhaustion of the day. The sentries maintained their watchful stance as they looked out on the alert for danger.

With these lingering observations, Vic fell asleep.

Over the next days, Vic once again settled in amidst the pattern and routine of a day in the life of a Beest. The Crossing was now a useful memory. On this side of the River, the grass was lush after the recent rains. The Herd moved contently and even lazily across the savannah. Life here was good.

Vic used his time wisely. With less urgency to find the next good meal and drink, Vic could really begin to meditate on what he had learned from the previous weeks. While he played with the other calves and encouraged some of the new orphans, Vic frequently took the time out to find a vantage point and to consider all he had learned so far. Sometimes, he took his view from another knoll; other times, it was atop a flat rocky outcropping. Sometimes, even the Edge proved to be useful. Such times and locations gave him the opportunity to watch and observe the Herd and the world around him.

Sometimes, Vic would look to the Horizon ahead and think deeply about his Vision of leading the Herd and about bringing all the plains' game together to a School of Success where they each would work together to improve the Circle of Life. As he did so, his Passion grew and, with that, his Commitment grew stronger.

The more he thought about his Vision, the more Vic could picture it, and the more he could picture it, the more he believed he would actually be able to achieve it. Although unaware, Vic was now creating new behaviors as a result; these behaviors would see him successfully through his Journey.

Vic knew now from his previous lessons with Men-taur that, when the time was right, Men-taur would appear. Since the Crossing, he had seen Men-taur predominantly in the company of other Beest, often with their heads together, often heading toward the leading edge of the Herd. Sometimes, Vic would follow. Occasionally, he caught Men-taur's eye, and Men-taur would nod a greeting but do so with a look that said, 'Keep back; not yet'. And so Vic became expectant of his next lesson, and became increasingly eager to learn and to grow. He began to wonder what the next lesson would be. He did not have to wait long...

This day, Vic was sheltering with a few other Beest under the shade of an acacia tree. The sun was burning hotly in the sky and was relentless in its purpose to bake everything it contacted. The shade provided some reprieve from the heat but not from the flies.
With his tail flicking with annoyance, Vic tried to beat back the hungry onslaught. It was a losing battle.

Then, through the shimmering haze of the day, Men-taur appeared, heading towards him. He was on his own. Vic quickly scrambled to his feet with excitement and expectation. Vic wondered how Men-taur always seemed to know how to find him in amongst such a large Herd. But that thought did not have time to linger.

Acknowledging the nods of the other Beest under the tree, Men-taur approached Vic. "So, Vic, how is my student today?"

"Fine, thank you, Men-taur. I am glad to see you," replied Vic.

"And I you. It has been some time now since the Crossing. Hopefully you have been using the time wisely to review your lessons so far and to apply what you have been learning?"

"Yes, I have. The more I think on what I have learned, the more the lessons interconnect," answered Vic.

"Funny that," said Men-taur. "Sounds like the time I have given you for reflection has proven useful."

"Yes it has," confirmed Vic.

"Good. Then before we progress on with today's lesson, as before, please remind me of the key things you learned from our lesson about Commitment as it relates to achieving your Vision on your Journey," requested Men-taur.

Because Vic had been reviewing and reflecting on what he had learned from his lesson on Commitment and, indeed, his lessons on Vision and Passion, he began his reply almost before Men-taur had finished his request.

"The Crossing emphasized my need for Commitment to get to the other side of the River. Once committed, I had to keep moving forwards in order to achieve my goal, and that equally applies to my own Commitment to achieving my Vision. While I succeeded in crossing the River, others did not; their failure was regrettably an opportunity to learn. In my future, in the event of failure, I must endeavor to stop and absorb the lesson, which will ultimately help me to grow."

"I went back to the River after the Crossing, and I saw the pain and the failure — mothers were seeking their calves, unfortunate Beest had been washed ashore and, perhaps the saddest, others were stuck on the other side, too afraid to cross."

"Indeed," said Men-taur.

"With your experience, help and guidance, I realized that, when I know the Journey is going to get tough, when there is a plan in advance which has milestones along the way, success is more likely," Vic added appreciatively.

Men-taur smiled.

When Vic noted that Men-taur was not going to say anything, he continued. "Also, as I achieve a milestone, I feel further energized and my Commitment increases on a much deeper and much more intense level. When I know my desired outcome and focus my energy consistently with Passion and Commitment, my Vision is more certain," concluded Vic.

"Very good, Vic. Very good. I'm glad to hear that what you have learned so far has begun to be ingrained," encouraged Men-taur with a big grin. "Now that we have confirmed that you are making the most of these lessons, Vic, it is time for us to move on to your fourth lesson," continued Men-taur. "And we will start with some points of further reflection regarding the Crossing."

The lessons had, by now, such a familiar pattern to Vic that he instinctively knew when to be quiet, when to respond and when to raise a question. Now was the part he enjoyed the most — the start of a new lesson. Vic had discovered that being both excited and expectant about these lessons meant that, when they finally arose, he was both ready for them and rewarded for his patience. He was sure the value of these lessons would stand the test of time; after all, they were being handed down from generation to generation of Beest — and he felt absolutely privileged to be part of that specific aspect of the Circle of Life for the Herd.

Something about Vic must have caught Men-taur's attention because Vic, once again, was brought back to the moment. "Vic... Vic!"

"Sorry, Men-taur. I was thinking about how privileged I am that you are giving me these lessons," replied Vic, and then quickly added, "I just want to say thank you for investing your valuable time, energy and interest to share your knowledge and experience with me."

Men-taur seemed to shift his weight from one front hoof to the other for a few seconds as though he was uncomfortable with the show of gratitude. "You are most welcome, Vic. Your progress so far is evidence that I have invested, as you put it, my time, energy, interest and knowledge wisely. You are a good student," paused Men-taur. "So, on that note, let's get back to you reflecting on what you have learned from the Crossing. Only this time I want you to think forward to the future, to a time when you will do another Crossing, and ask yourself an additional key question."

Vic remained still, and silently considered what the question could be.

"Normally, Vic, I ask two questions; you have answered the first question, which is 'What have I learned so far about a Crossing?'. You provided a positive summary of the last lesson and, therefore, a positive answer to the first question." Men-taur smiled for a moment. "The second question — which is an equally important question — is, 'What will I do differently or change the next time?'"

When Men-taur stopped speaking and left a very pregnant silence, Vic knew this was an indication that he was expected to fill the space. Vic decided to give this question some thought.

Men-taur just waited and, whilst he did, he dropped his head and ripped a few mouthfuls of the lush grass to chew on.

Finally, Vic responded, "I noticed on the Crossing that some Beest panicked. As a result, they created a chain reaction as they prematurely headed to the River many Beest behind them followed. The result was too many Beest all crushing together. And, from what I saw, this decision and panic caused injuries and some Beest were even trampled. With this in mind, the next time, maybe we could create a waiting zone at a safe distance from the River so that only one group at a time is at the River bank for their Crossing. Once one group is significantly across the River, then the next group could be ushered forward."

Vic paused to catch his breath and then added, "I believe that this would lead to less injuries and deaths and, therefore, fulfil your Vision, Men-taur, of getting many Beest safely around the Journey."

"I like that idea, Vic. I like how you have tied future plans into my Vision. Nicely done," said Men-taur reassuringly, before continuing. "Anything else?"

"Well, yes," replied Vic excitedly, relishing the praise from Men-taur, "there are a couple more changes I believe would be helpful for future Crossings."

"Go on," encouraged Men-taur.

So Vic added, "I noticed when we were crossing... well, actually, it was more when I played it back in my mind that I realized it had been easier for me to swim across when you were upstream of me, taking the fuller force of the River. In light of that, I think it would be a good idea to create a general rule, where adults cross on the upstream side of calves or the injured; I think this would again result in more reaching the opposite bank safely. We could even establish a 'buddy system' where everyone must cross with a buddy — especially orphans."

As Vic had stopped, Men-taur queried, "You said there were a couple more changes? What's the other change you would recommend?"

"Well, when I returned to the River afterwards," Vic added, "I noticed there were a few Beest stuck on the other side in distress; some were calves, some were cows, some were the elderly, and some were the frightened. Just because we cross the River alone and are thankful we crossed safely, why can we not take a Herd perspective and ask how can we help these stranded Beest to cross rather than leaving them on the other side at risk of being preyed upon by Lion and Hyena? Could we not assign a rescue team of the strongest and most experienced swimmers to return and help the remaining ones to cross?"

Men-taur quickly responded, "Vic, those are phenomenal ideas. You have given me much to think about regarding how we can potentially progress these ideas into something that is both practical and works successfully." Then, looking straight at Vic, Men-taur said simply, "It is my turn to thank you, Vic; you have really added some value to my day and to my leadership. A true leader humbly acknowledges the contributions of others."

Vic did not know where to look. If he had no hair on his face, Men-taur would have seen his face becoming flushed.

Men-taur then continued, "If you had not already figured out today's lesson, it is about Change - being prepared to Change and learn from that Change — both are inextricably linked. You have made a good start using your experience from the Crossing. Now, let's continue. To do what we need to do, we must take a walk," stated Men-taur. And with that he turned and headed out into the full heat of the day.

A true leader humbly acknowledges the contributions of others.

Vic quickly caught up. His curiosity was piqued and he was eager to ask Men-taur what the lesson was fully about, but he knew better; Men-taur would tell him at the appropriate moment. And so Vic contented himself with being in Men-taur's company.

Together, they walked for what seemed ages. Already, they had passed by what appeared to be the Edge. Feeling uneasy about being exposed and without the protection within the Herd, Vic began to truly wonder where they were headed.

Lesson 4 – Change & Learn

As they walked, Vic noticed that the grass at their feet, lush and rich from the recent rains, cushioned each step and actually made the walk easier compared to the hard-baked ground of recent months. Vic wished at that very moment that they could stay in this area forever; there seemed to be an abundance of water and lush grazing.

Vic was stirred from his reverie when Men-taur began to slow his pace. Ahead there was a broken stretch of acacia and bushes across their path. Vic became even more alert when a strange scent reached his nostrils. It was different to anything he had experienced before. He knew the smell of a Lion and a Hyena; he could differentiate the smell of a Giraffe from a Gazelle. This, however, was very different. Now, Vic began to feel a distinct unease and his heart began to pound more evidently in his chest.

Men-taur continued slowly for a few more paces before stopping. He appeared calm and assured, but his twitching ears, his silent tail and focused gaze ahead suggested otherwise.

Turning quietly toward Vic, Men-taur pursed his lips with a silent "Ssshhh!" and began to carefully approach the bushes from a different angle. At the same time, Vic picked up a sound on the wind which was, again, odd and felt out of place. It was an animal he had never heard before, and he was unable to compare it to anything.

"HEYAH! HEYAH!"

A broken chorus of animals seemed to bleat in response.

"HEYAH! HEYAH!"

Vic looked at Men-taur with a sense of alarm. The sound now seemed to be getting closer. His very being was screaming to get away as quickly as he could. Men-taur, sensing Vic's rising panic, shot him a brief but encouraging look.

Through a gap in the nearby bushes, a strange sight caught Vic's eyes. With a long pointed stick held in one leg, standing erect on another two legs, waving its other free leg with what looked like a detached tail, was the strangest animal he had ever seen in his short life.

Around this animal's feet was a small Herd of grazing animals. They seemed to be under the direction of the erect animal because every gesture it made, they moved in response.

Casting his eyes back to the erect animal, Vic noted how tall and thin it was.

"HEYAH! HEYAH!"

Vic's heart accelerated even more as, joining this strange animal, another similar animal came into view and headed towards the other. The animals had now turned to speak with each other. The bleating lowered and the grazing animals turned their interest to the grass beneath them and began to eat with quick, short bites.

When the animals had turned their backs to them, Men-taur motioned with his muzzle and slowly backed away with one eye on where he was going and the other on the strange animals. Vic needed no further prompting; he was glad to be moving, especially in the opposite direction to those animals.

Using the bushes and trees as cover, Men-taur and Vic retreated a good distance until they could only faintly hear the animals and their Herd. Eventually, reaching the shade of an acacia tree, Men-taur stopped but kept his eyes focused forward. Coming alongside Men-taur, Vic also stopped. Men-taur was breathing deeply and slowly. As he did so, Vic noted the tension seem to dissipate from Men-taur.

After some moments, Vic began to feel calmer, and then he noted that such was their vantage point, that they could both still see the animals and their Herd in the distance.

Men-taur turned his head toward Vic and began, "Vic, what you—"

"Men-taur, I'm sorry to interrupt but what were those animals?" questioned Vic hurriedly.

"Patience, Vic. Patience. I was coming to that before you interrupted. I will tell you what I know," reassured Men-taur.

"What you just saw was the animal called Man; Man is a very interesting species. Man is at the core of this part of your lesson today. Actually, before I continue, let's first head back to the Herd; it is not wise to stay outside of the fold of the Herd for too long — out here we are a bit exposed so we need to be cautious of predators." Men-taur paused and then asked, "How do you feel about not being within the Herd right now, Vic?"

As he began to trot away, Men-taur shot one last look at the Man to ensure nothing of significance had changed in what they were doing, and then turned and headed back towards where the Herd were located.

Alongside, Vic replied, "Well, as we were heading out here, I felt very uneasy; I felt wary and edgy because I've always been taught there is safety in numbers back in the Herd. Out here, we would be easier targets for a Lion. Then, when I saw and smelled the Man, I became more concerned, uncomfortable and even afraid. It reminded me of the night I got separated from my mom."

With that confession, Vic went quiet as he reflected on missing his mother; he had not really thought of her for a while and felt guilty as a result.

Men-taur kept silent, allowing some time for Vic to reflect. As he did so, Men-taur began scanning the way before them and allowed the gap of silence to take root before he finally responded, "That is to be expected, Vic. You had a normal reaction to being outside the Herd and the comfort of its protection. Most of us like to stay inside the Herd and the comfort that brings and, as such, we will never truly

experience Change," continued Men-taur, "When confronted with
Change, we often want to maintain things as they are because we are
afraid of Change. In some instances, this manifests as a resistance to
the Change. For example, let's take our experience with the Man.
I knew they were out here. I knew it would be too much to bring the
Herd too close to them because many in the Herd would panic because
Man is something 'new'. So, I instead chose to take a calculated risk
with you, Vic, and decided we should seek to find Man together
so that you could better understand your lesson. In fact, it is worth
emphasizing that risk is a harbinger of change."

...risk is a harbinger of change.

"Out here, outside our comfort zone, there is the opportunity to
Change and the opportunity to grow. The Herd will generally not see
Change as a growth opportunity; their fear and resistance to Change
will hold them back from finding their true purpose on their Journey.
Understand this, Vic," stressed Men-taur, "Change is inevitable;
growth is optional. So, for each Beest to truly grow, they must be
prepared to Change."

"Understand also, Vic, that the Journey is an accepted Change from
generations past; if we opted not to travel the Journey, the threat of a
lack of food and water becomes real and Beest subsequently die;
as such, sometimes the pain and fear which would result from not
changing are strong motivators to actually bringing about Change. It is
important to realize that Change is Nature, and Nature includes Change."

Vic contemplated Men-taur's words before listening to
Men-taur continue.

"Consider the season the Herd is a part of now," Men-taur
suggested, "Mothers are now beginning to wean off their calves; this
is a Change which must happen. It is inevitable. Of course, like much
Change, it is uncomfortable and can even be painful for both the calf
and the mother. In particular, the calf is being forced into a new and
necessary experience. At times, it may even feel afraid — afraid of the
unknown and afraid of losing what is familiar. However, without the
gradual process of weaning, the calf cannot truly grow and realize the

pleasure of being an adult in the Herd, and the mother's body cannot prepare sufficiently for the birth of the next calf. In order to make the process less painful, cows allow these calves to stick by them until such a time when the new calf is born. By then, the calf has then become accustomed to the new way of things and has increasingly ventured away from the proximity of its mother."

Change is inevitable; growth is optional.

Men-taur seemed to realize that he had been speaking for some time, and so he looked to Vic. "Are you with me so far, Vic?"

"Yes, Men-taur," replied Vic.

"Good. Now why do you think I took you all the way to see the Man?" asked Men-taur.

All Vic could think of was that it had something to do with Man but he could not see it in his mind yet. However, he did answer, "Well, I suppose that Man is an animal we need to be wary of and even avoid if possible."

"Exactly. To avoid Man, however, will be difficult. The reason I brought you out here is to emphasize this lesson. Man is here to stay. Man is causing concern for all of the various animals here on the plain. During each Journey, Man shows up earlier and in greater numbers with their Herds; their Herds do not mix with ours and their Herds seem to be increasing in number. Nevertheless, our leaders and those of the Gazelle, Zebra and others here have also noted that the Journey's boundaries are becoming more and more restricted as Man is encroaching on our territory. Man's Herds are competing for the same food we seek, and so we seem to need to keep moving at all times when, in the past, we would have some time to enjoy it here longer."

Vic was beginning to see ahead into the future so, as Men-taur took a breath to scan the Horizon, he asked, "So, with Man ahead of us, we must make a decision to change our course to avoid coming into contact with Man?"

"That's right, Vic. An astute leader will always be able to discern the signs, adjust or Change, and take action accordingly, which is always in the best interests of the Herd," agreed Men-taur.

Vic added, "And without making that Change to the course in our Journey, we may become endangered on two sides — Man ahead of us and Lion behind us for example. The threat to us increases so we must find another way around this area."

Vic was becoming increasingly more confident in voicing his understanding.

By now they had returned to the Edge. Both Men-taur and Vic slowed their pace almost simultaneously as they passed through a group of grazing Beest being watched over by a bull sentry.

"You are right once again, Vic," agreed Men-taur with a nod, "We are now in a situation where there is a fork in the path before us: We can either proceed as we have done and come up against Man and all the uncertainties that brings, or we can otherwise choose to determine another route through this area, giving a wide berth to the Man and his Herd," considered Men-taur.

At this point, Men-taur paused and beckoned to the bull sentry who then walked over to meet both Men-taur and Vic. Men-taur then relayed the message about Man and the need to coordinate the movement of the Herd away from the area. Once he had checked that the other bull understood what needed to be done, Men-taur returned his attention to Vic.

Walking deeper into the Herd, they stopped beneath a lone acacia tree. It was a welcome respite from the direct sun, which had been relentlessly beating upon them.

"Take this acacia seedling here," said Men-taur, motioning to the small plant which seemed to originate from under the small boulder next to where they were standing. "As you can see, it is growing from just under that small overhang on this boulder. I am guessing that, somehow, a seed from this tree overhead managed to get lodged here, possibly during some heavy rains. As you can see, its small trunk has had to bend, and so it had to make the decision to either follow a path of least resistance and make a Change to its course of growth, or to stop growing once it hit the rock and, thereby, threaten its survival. It learned to change direction based on the feedback from its surrounding environment. In addition, it had faith to make that Change believing that to do so was the better option."

Men-taur gave Vic a moment to consider the teachings. "We are having to take a similar path," Men-taur finally continued, "We are taking the feedback of what we discovered this afternoon and using it to plot a new course with the least resistance which will aid our progress through this area. Interestingly, where were we in relation to the Herd when we were able to gain that insight, Vic?"

"We were ahead of it," replied Vic.

"And, knowing we were exposed out there and how we felt, what would be another name for where we were?" questioned Men-taur.

"Our Comfort Zone," answered Vic quickly, as he made some mental connections.

"Exactly. Only at the Edge and beyond your Comfort Zone do you truly acquire the necessary feedback you need in order to be able to make the key decisions which will ultimately lead to your success. That is where true lessons take place and where you will be able to gain a wealth of vitally helpful information to assimilate and use to expand your Comfort Zone. Remember though Vic that out beyond your Comfort Zone is where both fear and opportunity can exist; which one you choose to focus on solely depends on your outlook."

Men-taur took a moment to think and then smiled down at Vic. "Beyond your Comfort Zone is your Success Zone," emphasized Men-taur. "And so, becoming a true success is dependent on the size of your Comfort Zone; expand your Comfort Zone and you will expand your Success Zone."

Vic smiled and took a breath; he was feeling optimistic and excited about the future, about his Vision, and about his learning with Men-taur.

> *Only at the Edge and beyond our Comfort Zone*
> *do you truly acquire the necessary feedback*
> *you need in order to be able to make*
> *the key decisions which will ultimately*
> *lead to your success.*

"Vic, it is worth sharing that those lessons which arise when you are expanding your Comfort Zone can often come as a direct result of failure to make the right decision and/or failure to get the result you were expecting," continued Men-taur. "However, there is common saying here on the plains that, 'failure is only feedback'; my own preferred way of explaining it is that F.A.I.L.U.R.E is *Focused And Insightful Learning Using Real Experience*," expanded Men-taur.

"In fact, success often arises from failure. Failure is a part of life; it is a way of knowing you are living. Living is only a series of real experiences; a series of learnings," concluded Men-taur.

F.A.I.L.U.R.E is Focused And Insightful Learning Using Real Experience

Men-taur allowed Vic time to absorb what he had divulged — and Vic certainly needed some time. For Vic, today's lesson had felt strangely different to the ones he had previously undertaken. Perhaps it was due to having so much to learn, and he knew that in today's lesson was an answer to a question he had not yet thought of.

Men-taur continued to stand attentively. The Herd was slowing its pace as the Beest lazily grazed roundabout. Vic began to wonder if any of them thought much about what was beyond the Herd.

Vic allowed the soundscape of the savannah to wash over him as he sorted through all of the information in his mind. As time was progressing now towards dusk, the nocturnal insect denizens were beginning their chorus. The thrum was soothing; the rhythm relaxing. Vic's thoughts began to collate.

Seeing that Vic's brow had become less furrowed with thought, Men-taur prompted, "Now seems a good time to summarize what you have learned today."

Vic took a few slow breaths and absorbed the pulse of life around him. He felt grateful to be at this point in time with Men-taur, and felt in harmony with the surroundings, in harmony with Men-taur and in harmony with the lesson. Out of this brief meditation Vic began. "Today's lesson was about Change and being prepared to learn. Unlike in previous lessons, today, Men-taur, you exposed me to several opportunities to learn from my past experiences, my current ones and future possible ones that could arise. From a past experience, such as the Crossing, I can ask myself some key questions to first establish what

I learned and then what I would change about a similar experience if it arose again.

"When we headed out from the Herd and saw the animal called Man, I was outside of my Comfort Zone, which I now see is both a place of fear and a place of opportunity. Outside my Comfort Zone I am taking a risk, and taking a risk often suggests that change is coming. Some risks are actually necessary in order to truly experience the effects of Change and to get the beneficial feedback required to make effective decisions which enable us to adapt our Journey ahead for our own good and that of others."

Vic paused to catalogue his thoughts. In the brief moment that took, Men-taur just nodded encouragingly, and so Vic continued. "As with the example of calves now being weaned across the Herd, those calves— or any other Beest who resists change — will likely not realize their purpose on the Journey. It is these Beest who will not experience growth, for Change is inevitable but growth is optional. Change brings learning and that means we increase our Success Zone."

Vic stopped.

Men-taur waited for a moment to determine whether Vic was going to continue before asking, "And how does failure fit into all of this?"

Vic winced inwardly, chastising himself for incorrectly thinking he had successfully recalled everything. With a tone of remorse, Vic apologized, "Sorry, Men-taur, I thought I had remembered everything."

"There's no need to apologize, Vic," smiled Men-taur, "Apologies fit best when you have truly erred; you have only to add this part of your summary, and all is forgotten." Men-taur purposefully left an encouraging space hanging in the air for Vic to fill.

In response, Vic quickly stepped in, "When failure occurs, it is an opportunity to learn because, from the learning can arise future successes. As you said, Men-taur, 'Failure stands for *Focused and Insightful Learning Using Real Experience.*' Failure provides all with an opportunity to change and, as change is inevitable, so often is failure. Out of failure comes growth." As Vic finished, it seemed the awakening nightlife around added its supportive chorus of chirps, buzzes and hums.

After a moment, Men-taur added his encouragement, "Well done again, Vic. Once again you have gleaned the nuggets of the lesson well."

Vic felt elated.

"Now," directed Men-taur, "keep those nuggets and the other lessons on Vision, Passion and Commitment to heart. Continue to integrate each of these essential learnings into what you experience and, therefore, what you learn each day. Do so, Vic, and you will grow stronger in your purpose and more in harmony with the Rhythm; do so and the Circle of Life will feed back to you what you need to fulfil as your part of the Journey. And remember, in the days ahead — and for always — be prepared for Change and to Change."

Vic nodded in response.

"Now, the Herd has gone without me for long enough. With Man ahead of us, I must make sure that the Herd is prepared to adjust its path. It is time for me to go, Vic. When the Herds begin to converge again, I'll come and find you," concluded Men-taur.

...be prepared for Change and to Change.

Men-taur then turned toward the night. The lesson was now over and Vic knew and understood far more than he had at sun-up that day. Feeling more knowledgeable and enthusiastic, Vic really felt blessed to have gleaned more practical knowledge, and felt excited both by what he had learned about Change and the reassurance that there would be a further lesson.

Men-taur called out from the night, "Remember to look at every experience ahead of you under the light of the lessons so far. Your growth will accelerate when you do."

"Nothing is permanent but change....
It is in changing that things find purpose."

Heraclitus

"One of the most difficult things is not to change
society - but to change yourself."

Nelson Mandela

Exercise 4 - **Your Preparedness to Change and Learn**

As with the previous exercises, please consider this exercise carefully and thoughtfully, as it pertains to successfully achieving your Vision that you noted previously.

1. On a scale of 1-10*, how strong is your level of preparedness to Change and learn for the Vision that you wrote down for Exercise 1? _____

2. In the event that you scored yourself below an 8, what 3 things do you need to be and/or do which will help to increase your preparedness to Change and learn to achieve your Vision to an 8+?

    _____

    _____

    _____

    _____

    _____

    _____

    _____

    _____

    _____

    _____

    _____

    _____

    _____

    _____

    _____

* For this and the other exercises, please note that a score of 1 represents the weakest and a score of 10 represents the strongest.

Chapter Eight

"In every success story, you find someone who has made a courageous decision."

Peter F. Drucker

"It doesn't matter which side of the fence you get off on sometimes. What matters most is getting off. You cannot make progress without making decisions."

Jim Rohn

Since coming across Man, the days had begun to blur into one for Vic. The Herd continued its Journey and was always moving. On some days, the Herd moved longer into the dusk and even continued deep into the night. There was the speculation amongst the Beest that this was due to an animal known as Man. Whilst Vic knew that the longer days of travel were as a result of giving Man a wide berth to avoid direct contact, the majority of Beest had either no interest in the truth or otherwise had chosen to focus on what was before them — or not.

The increasing focus of discussion or, rather complaining, as Vic called it, surrounded the now daily difficulties of the lengthening treks, the decreasing quality and availability of good grazing, and the lack of good watering holes to drink from and bathe in. Although Vic originally tried to impart his knowledge from his experiences and lessons with Men-taur, he was mostly frowned upon as an "impudent, cock-sure youth who liked to sound important and mature beyond his years," as proclaimed some of the adults with an audience. This usually brought about a chuckle of laughter from the collected Beest with a cumulative message of dismissal on the faces of those gathered.

Fortunately, being ostracized from such negatives groups of Beest did not bother Vic; he found all the company he needed amongst the many thoughts surrounding his lessons and with the growing excitement and expectation of more lessons with Men-taur. Vic, therefore, soon decided it was wise for him to keep his mouth closed and keep his thoughts to himself, even when he took time to mix with the other youth. On occasion, however, he did find a listening ear and, on the occasions when he did, he took the opportunity to vocalize and share his lessons, as a whole or in part. In particular, Vic took to heart Men-taur's last parting words, "Remember to look at every experience ahead of you under the light of the lessons so far. Your growth will accelerate when you do."

So, throughout each day, Vic took time to ponder his lessons and to apply all he had learned from them to each day's experiences. After all, to Vic, each day was a day of discovery.

Vic saw Men-taur sparingly. Rarely, did much in the way of words pass between them such were the demands on Men-taur's time.

Eventually, the Journey began to become numbing and wearing. The savannah became drier, the grazing thinner, the waterholes smaller and the days longer and thus more tiring. As a result, the level of complaining amongst the Herd began to grow, and even Vic's enthusiasm for each new day wavered with the constant onslaught of negativity from the Herd.

And then it finally started — the rain. It came at first as a mere trickle and then progressively got heavier. Vic woke shaking his head; rain was irritatingly managing to find its way into his left ear. It was a welcome change to the dust and dampened the impact of the foreboding heat of recent days.

Like Vic, the other Beest were awakening from a night of dreamless sleep after another long trek the previous day. Looking around him, Vic could see that, judging from the initial reactions, the Herd had welcomed the rain after only a fleeting annoyance. Some Beest even uncharacteristically gadded about like newborn calves. Vic concluded that pleasure often comes from the simpler things and only a few recognize the joy of the moment.

With that thought in mind, Vic sprung to his feet and joined in with those jubilating over the rain. As he did, he heard one spry elder cow exclaim breathlessly after a spate of gadding, "Rain means life and life is good".

Vic smiled and lifted his head into the rain so that he could feel the raindrops fall more squarely upon his face. He spent a few moments in reverie using all his senses to soak up the rain and its impact on the life around him. Every sound seemed to be flooded out as his thoughts coalesced in harmony with his surroundings. Vic felt that he could truly feel the Earth's Rhythm, and it made him feel elated and in harmony with every element.

"BBBBOOOOMMMMMM!!!"

Thunder rapidly split the silence and the sky blazed a blinding white.

The joyful moment evaporated. Not only did the sound and brightness startle Vic but also the other Beest nearby. In its place all the Beest became noticeably uneasy — storms often had that effect. The rain now had turned into a downpour. Every Beest was now beginning to lower their heads to avoid being pelted by bigger and bigger drops of rain.

As Vic lowered his head, that was when he saw Men-taur.

Men-taur nodded Vic over with an economy of motion. Indeed, there was no point in trying to speak because of the noise of the rain.

Once within a few paces of each other, Men-taur greeted Vic, "Morning, Vic."

"Good morning, Men-taur," Vic replied enthusiastically.

"Normally, I would add a 'Good' to that, but I'll reserve that until the rain stops," smiled Men-taur.

Vic smiled back feeling, once again, that resurging excitement now that he was in Men-taur's company. Vic knew that he was about to enter another lesson.

"So, Vic, are you ready for your next lesson?" queried Men-taur.

"Yes, Men-taur," confirmed Vic.

"Good. Fortuitously, today's rain will probably play a significant part," added Men-taur cryptically.

As always, Vic felt a swelling curiosity, and so he asked a question, actually two questions in rapid succession that materialized on his lips, "What is today's lesson? And how does the rain fit in?"

"Well, Vic," shouted Men-taur as another roll of thunder boomed across their path, "those are two very good questions that I will address in due time. Now, however, as with your previous lessons, we will summarize your last lesson and any further insights you have gained since then. But, before we do that, let's walk; that way the rain has to hit a moving target." Men-taur chuckled with his last comment and then headed off with his head bowed, walking against the rain.

In fact, the Herd had changed direction a few days after the encounter with Man. To Vic, that now seemed such a long time ago. Each morning since had been consistently greeted with the sun beating down on him and the rest of the Herd as soon as it crested the Horizon. Today was a refreshing change with the onslaught of the rain and, whilst the Journey continued, any change broke the monotony of heat-filled days.

Vic quietly continued alongside Men-taur as they picked their way through the thickening mud. Dour faces of other Beest turned their way unimpressed by the rain. Vic kept quiet. He sensed that Men-taur wanted to get somewhere before they could actually start the lesson.

Finally, they began to climb a hill. As they approached the top Vic noticed two things: A flat-topped boulder, and the view ahead falling away abruptly.

Men-taur headed to the lee of the boulder directly before them. In that space several Beest could probably have fit. For now, however, it was a luxurious bubble of protection from the rain that, until seconds before, had been driving into them.

Just as Men-taur started to speak the rain all round began to thin out and fade.

"Now isn't that typical! I go to this effort to find shelter and then we don't need it!" Men-taur said, chuckling with mock annoyance. "I have learned to find the humor in most things, Vic. It seems our Creator has a sense of humor too!"

Vic smiled but rather than pay too much attention to Men-taur's jokes, Vic instead stared intently, awaiting the beginning of the lesson.

"Now, Vic, it seems that you have been given a natural platform to summarize your last lesson, so over to you," said Men-taur.

Before answering, Vic took advantage of the lessening rain to quickly shake off his sodden coat. The rainwater sprayed out in a sweeping arc in all directions — with some even splattering Men-taur's face.

With a sudden realization of what he had just done, Vic's eyes sprang open and he blurted out mortified, "Sorry, Men-taur!"

Men-taur looked sternly at Vic and held his gaze for what seemed ages. Then, what Vic mistook for the initial rumblings of distant thunder, Men-taur let out a bellow that resonated into an uncontrollable laugh.

Vic was initially confused, but when Men-taur winked at him in the midst of his raucous laughter, Vic joined in .

After some time, both seemed to recapture a modicum of dignity and, slowly, their laughter simmered into the odd chuckle.

"My goodness, Vic, I have not had a good laugh like that in a while," confessed Men-taur. "The look of sheer panic and anxiety on your face when you realized you had sprayed me was priceless. I couldn't help myself!"

"Oh, Men-taur, I truly am sorry. I never intended to get you wetter than you already were! Clearly, I wasn't thinking," Vic sincerely apologized.

"Ah, never mind, Vic. It is always good to take responsibility for your actions but I won't hold your transgression against you!" Men-taur replied with another wink.

"Now, let's get back to the question I asked and the answer you have yet to give," emphasized Men-taur. As always, Men-taur leveled his gaze at Vic when he expected a reply and then just waited.

Clearing his mind of his faux pas, Vic stated, "You had just asked me to summarize my previous lesson."

Men-taur nodded.

Vic quickly filled the deepening silence with his response, "The last lesson was focused on the importance and inevitability of Change and the necessity of always being prepared to learn, whether it be from past or current experiences and even the anticipation of future ones. Change and growth are interconnected. Regardless of the experience, it is also necessary to ask relevant questions in order to clarify what has been learned and what could be changed or done in the future when faced with similar circumstances." Vic paused, expecting a response from Men-taur, but Men-taur merely raised his eyebrows encouragingly, and so Vic continued. "When we came across Man we did so outside the confines of the Herd and outside of my Comfort Zone. Outside my Comfort Zone there is a risk, and with risk often comes Change. From that experience, we gained information, feedback and learning that you then used to make an effective decision for the benefit of the entire Herd regarding the future route of the Journey to take the Herd around Man. Ultimately, that decision is for the ongoing success of the Herd, the Journey and your Vision." Vic took a big breath before continuing, "Finally, learning can often arise from failure which stands for 'Focused and Insightful Learning Using Real Experience'. When that learning is applied it often enhances the likelihood of future success."

"Very good, Vic. Very good," acknowledged Men-taur. Men-taur then headed back the way they came without further comment. Vic no longer questioned any of Men-taur's actions, but instead just fell in step beside Men-taur. He knew the lesson was imminent; he had learned to be patient — even though his excitement bubbled away ferociously.

They left the shelter of the boulder and trotted back down the small hill. Once at the bottom they almost turned back on themselves and headed in the direction the Herd were now traveling. Because the ground had been so dry, the deluge of rain had turned the dust to mud. As such, the going became slower and, at times, slippery where the Herd had kneaded the ground into a thick sticky dough.

Their progress slowed even as they skirted along the edge of the slowly advancing Herd. Vic noted that most of the Beest were now mud-splattered, but there appeared to be a lightness of spirit which had been absent before the rain.

As they continued along, Vic did pick up the occasional comment from the Herd that with the rain had come hope and there was now the expectation of more water to drink and, hopefully, greener and lusher grazing ahead. That thought took seed in Vic's mind and he too felt happier with the thought of more plentiful water and mouthfuls of green, refreshing grass.

"Ehhhemm," snorted Men-taur.

As on occasions before, Vic was brought back from his reverie.

"Vic, are you with me?" Men-taur questioned as they reached the forward limits of the Herd.

"Yes, Men-taur," Vic said with a deferring tone. He now knew an apology or explanation for his daydreaming was likely not required; what Men-taur now wanted was his attention.

"Good. Now I want you to pay attention as your next lesson is about to commence. However, what the lesson is I will this time leave for you to discern. It is time for me to start weaning you off the milk so you can learn to gain more from the experience and from the lessons." Men-taur paused and then asked pointedly, "Is that understood?"

"Yes," Vic replied. Vic suddenly felt that his lessons had just taken a significant turn; a turn for what, he could not be sure.

"Right, Vic. I have an assignment for you," stated Men-taur. Men-taur waited to gauge how that statement impacted Vic.

Vic, at the same time, looked questioningly at Men-taur. While he could feel his stomachs drop and begin churning a little more than usual, Vic nevertheless felt a surge of excitement. Now he understood the turn his lessons had just taken — well, at least, in part anyway.

Satisfied both by what he saw and heard as well as what he didn't, Men-taur continued, "Vic, you have progressed through the lessons so far exceeding my expectations. With each lesson you have developed an insight and understanding beyond the years of most other Beest. Your progress has continued to confirm I made the right decision to take you as my student. Truly, you are a student of the Rhythm."

Vic smiled uneasily, still feeling uncomfortable of praise and unsure as to how to respond to such positive comments.

Men-taur then continued, "Now it's time, Vic, for you to shoulder some responsibility. Over the past several moons that we have been together, you have learned well and grown in both insight and understanding, and also in physical stature. As such, your lessons will arise from what you will now learn from this responsibility. You will be responsible for the task, and for the decisions and actions which you choose to take in order to complete this task. Am I making myself clear?" queried Men-taur.

"Yes, Sir!" Vic replied with zeal.

"Good. Vic, the assignment I have for you is within your capabilities," affirmed Men-taur. "It will require you to draw on what you have learned so far and it will stretch you to learn even more about yourself, the Journey, the Herd and what's on the Horizon."

Men-taur paused momentarily. "Vic, what I need you to do is to be a scout for the Herd for the foreseeable future; you will know when your task is complete," stated Men-taur.

Vic knew by the way Men-taur made that last statement that Men-taur was not expecting to be questioned.

"Generally, we are heading in the right direction," Men-taur continued. "We generally follow a similar Cycle on the Journey; however, because of the detours we have had to make in order to safely avoid Man, we are now on a part of the plains which is unfamiliar to the Herd. This is, therefore, unchartered territory. With this in mind, for the sake of the Herd, I need you to venture ahead to and beyond the Edge in order to establish the best and safest route; the route which has the best supply of water and grazing."

Allowing several heartbeats of time for Vic to absorb what he had just been assigned, Men-taur checked, "Is your assignment understood, Vic?"

"Yes, Men-taur," came Vic's simple reply.

The fact that Men-taur had assured and affirmed him bolstered Vic's courage. Even without knowing the fullness of what he was committing to, Vic felt encouraged and intent on completing his task to the best of his ability. After all, this lesson was not just for his benefit but was, perhaps most importantly, for the good of the Herd.

"What questions, if any, do you have, Vic?" asked Men-taur.

"Only one comes to mind immediately Men-taur: How am I to report back to you?"

"Good question," Men-taur assured and then responded, "It is best for you to report back at the end of the day to either myself or to one of the lead sentries on the Edge. In the event that there is something of particular importance you believe we must know about, report back immediately: Remember, to be forewarned is to be prepared. In the event that you do not report back at the end of a day, we will know that something troublesome has happened to you and we will act accordingly," added Men-taur ominously.

After a silent gulp at that last statement, Vic asked, "Can I also ask, Men-taur, what key things do you want me to be on the watch for?" Vic was keen to have clarity on the limits of his responsibilities.

"Another good question," Men-taur answered. "Part of your responsibility is to help locate the best grazing and places at which the Herd can get their fill of water. In addition, you must also locate where is the best place for the Herd to bed down for the night. You must come back when the sun is soon to drop below the Horizon, which will give us sufficient time to prepare the Herd. Now, is there anything else, Vic?" asked Men-taur.

Vic did not feel the need to respond; he was too preoccupied with trying to slow his racing heart as the significance of this task and its responsibility began to dawn on him.

Men-taur took the silence as a nil response. "You will do fine, Vic. I have every confidence in you. Now, there is no time like the present to get started — remember, it is the starting that often stops us; the Beest who deliberates too long before taking a step, will spend his entire life on three legs. "

Vic felt compelled to get started without the prompt from Men-taur. Because Vic had been with Men-taur often at or near the Edge and because he had been present at times when Men-taur had met with other scouts, Vic had a good idea of what was ahead of him. So with that he set off. All he did was nod silently to Men-taur as he passed by.

Remember, it is the starting that often stops us; the Beest who deliberates too long before taking a step, will spend his entire life on three legs.

With each step Vic felt the weight of the responsibility begin to bear down upon him; already he knew that it would take some getting used to.

The day was before him and his task was clear — it was time to embrace the moment, shoulder the responsibility and make the most of it. Vic knew he now had a new lesson to learn and, if he didn't start, he would stop. Vic took his responsibility very seriously. He knew that, because Men-taur had put a lot of faith in him, he had to fulfil this task to the best of his ability.

Dutifully, he reported back to Men-taur or one of the lead sentries over the ensuing days. His conversations with Men-taur and the sentries were restricted to what he had seen or heard beyond the Edge; they were very astute with their questions. They seemed to extract every last titbit of information from Vic so that they were able to make the right decisions for the Herd's welfare. On occasion, they needed even more information, which subsequently put Vic at further risk, but he would venture out once again to glean those last essential morsels of information.

Through this period, Vic's senses heightened. As he was exposed at times and, therefore, vulnerable to attack, Vic was always on the alert for signs of Lion, Hyena, Leopard and Hunting Dog. He tended to venture far enough ahead as his courage and his instinct would allow but, when the land behind him was broken and he could not see or hear the Herd in the distance, he shortened his range. He also memorized landmarks and what he thought were the surest and safest escape routes back to the Herd. In addition, where possible, he took to the higher ground or found a hidden vantage point which enabled him to see and — when the wind was right — smell — what lay ahead.

On two occasions over the past days his caution and instinct had saved him from walking into a pride of Lions. On another occasion, his escape route preparation, complete with purposeful obstacles, had saved him from a prowling Leopard amongst a thicket of acacia trees. It also helped that his fitness and strength were increasing as he grew in age, stature and experience.

The hardest part of the scouting was trying to locate sufficient water to provide for the Herd. Water, at this point of the Journey, was still a limited resource and, as every animal on the plain needed water to survive, it would be in high demand and short supply. Every animal knew this, whether they were prey or predator, and so with water subsequently came the potential for danger. In order to try to minimize the danger, Vic knew he had to make the right decisions in response to a series of questions:

Do I need more information to know if this is the right place for us to water the Herd?

Does the need of the Herd outweigh the risk to the Herd?

When is the right time for me to head back to the Herd?

When is the right time for the Herd to approach this watering hole?

What unforeseen dangers might arise in the interim?

What direction should we best approach it from?

Vic had progressively begun to anticipate the questions from Men-taur and the sentries. With such considerations in mind, the more information Vic could gather pertaining, particularly, to any potential water source, the better. Vic knew, the more information he could gather, the more it helped him to make better decisions. As time progressed, Vic could sense and smell water with increasing accuracy. Using all the information he could glean from these sensory perceptions, Vic could begin to make decisions faster and more effectively which ultimately satisfied the purpose of benefiting the Herd. Through this experience, Vic became more intent on serving the Herd and was less focused on himself.

Times arose when the Herd did lose Beest along the way. Often, the attacks came along the flanks of the Herd at dusk or dawn or at a watering hole. On a couple of occasions, the attacks came from an unexpected direction. Crocodile lay beneath the surface of the water close to the water's edge; the recent increase of rainstorms had swollen some of the watering holes. That had allowed the Crocodile to get very close and to suddenly explode from the water so that, before any other Beest knew it, a startled Beest had been dragged below the surface.

"Risk cannot be avoided — only minimized," thought Vic. Still, this did not stop Vic from feeling responsible. After all, he had been the one who had contributed — at least in part — to a decision which had ultimately led to such events occurring.

Risk cannot be avoided — only minimized.

A new day arose with a shade of gray. There was no real dawn; only a progressive lessening of the darkness. The sun was nowhere to be seen. It had rained heavily all night. From days ago, when the new rain was welcomed with calf-like joy, it was now a source of complaint and grumbling. Not only were spirits dampened, but the ground was now so saturated that there really was no challenge for Vic to locate water — it was in seasonal abundance.

Now, however, the challenge for Vic was to help find enough grazing land which hadn't been pummeled into the mud. The Herd had been advancing ahead of the other Herds of Zebra and Gazelle in order to get to comparatively untrampled ground where the grass would be intact and, perhaps, only weather-beaten.

Listening once again to the rising complaints about the rain, grazing and general air of fatigue resulting from the seemingly endless trekking, Vic decided it was time to go. As he had been huddled on the Edge, it did not take him long to break free from the negative energy emanating from the Herd. The weather had, in fact, begun to take its toll on Vic too and, to be with other Beest who would only add to that soggy attitude, was not an option.

Receiving a nod of encouragement and a raised right hoof of salute from a nearby sentry, Vic set out at a reasonably quick pace; to go any faster meant an increased uncertainty of footing and a subsequent distraction from the task at hand and the awareness which it required.

Out here, his head cleared fast because he needed to focus all of his senses and apply his previous lessons and experience. Now, he was in what had become familiar territory. Out here in his Success Zone, as Men-taur had called it, he felt more alive and more attuned to his Vision and the Rhythm of Life. Out here he was alone with his thoughts and his wits. Out here was the test. Out here was his future.

Vic had been walking for some time on automatic, taking in landmarks and checking his progress with the occasional brief reference to the direction he had come from but with an intent focus on what lay ahead. Knowing that the state of the ground was a factor he had to take into consideration in the case of the need to escape, Vic kept his range closer this day. As he had grown in experience, this range was, however, at least double what it had been on the first day he had assumed his scouting role. Had others been with him, some would have said he was bold and others would have called him foolish. Regardless, it was Vic's decision to make.

Just when Vic was feeling perhaps overly confident, he noticed an ominous rumbling sound. It was different to that of the thunder to which he had become accustomed. Subsequently, he felt strangely uneasy. The wind had been coming from behind him and he began to berate himself for not paying more attention. He glanced around nervously.

Despite his quickened heart rate, he managed to maintain a methodical assessment of his surroundings. Scanning the surroundings for movement or anything out of the ordinary, he stood still with each leg slightly bent to allow for quick acceleration, with his ears forward to pick up the slightest sound, with his nose raised to catch the wind and with his eyes relatively unfocused to maximize the acuity of his peripheral vision.

After collating the information his environment was feeding him, Vic proceeded cautiously. Gauging the pace of the grazing Herd behind, Vic felt it necessary to maintain his pace, not wishing to increase the distance from where he was to relative safety back amongst the Herd. His curiosity was egging him on, but his discipline and innate sense of self-preservation won out.

On the Horizon before him was a line of stunted trees. Somehow, Vic knew when he got there his curiosity would be satisfied and so, with the wind behind him, he increased the frequency of looking briefly over his shoulders to ensure his distance from the Herd, his route back and his safety from any attack. The wind hindered his ability to locate the source or true direction of the sound. The only thing he was almost sure of was that the sound was coming from somewhere ahead.

Vic continued forward with his nerves on edge and his heart pounding fast and erratically. Adrenaline pumped through every cell of his body.

It seemed to take ages for Vic to reach that line of trees. As he approached, the rumbling began to transform into a deafening roar that even caused the ground to tremble. In the flicker of a moment, understanding dawned on Vic. As he crested the slight rise on which the trees were aligned, he knew what he would find before him: a raging swollen River in full flood.

Compared to his first Crossing, this River was seemingly fuller, angrier and more powerful. Fleetingly, Vic felt a glimmer of fear — not so much for himself but rather for the Herd; the Herd that was now tired and somewhat demoralized. As with before, the Crossing requires focus, commitment and physical exertion, and Vic already instinctively knew that this time would be a far greater challenge than that of before.

Vic knew this was what Men-taur had meant when he said he would know when the task of being a scout had come to a conclusion. However, before it could conclude, Vic knew that in order to save time and lives, he had to ideally find a suitable place for the Crossing. Equally, he knew that he should not venture too far beyond his range.

Vic stood still. He opened up the fullness of his senses and brought to mind all the lessons and the recollections of his past Crossing in a way to determine which way to look first — upstream or downstream. Where he had come upon the River, the bank was just a sheer drop down into it, and would probably be better described as a gorge. The River seemed to have cut out a path from the very rock.

Vic waited and breathed— deeply. His mind cleared; his heart slowed; his guts told him to head upstream. And so he did. His intuition had been heightened out here beyond the Edge. Success and intuition often go hand in hand.

Vic had to stay reasonably close to the edge of the gorge so that he could assess both sides of the River. As such, he had to tread carefully and allow himself enough room to maneuver to allow for a quick escape should the need arise.

At the limits of what he was going to allow himself, Vic noted the River took a sharp turn in the direction of the setting sun. As it did so, he noted that the depth of the gorge rapidly decreased.

At this point he noted three things. Firstly, just after the bend, the River here had narrowed considerably. Secondly, because of the sharpness of the bend, the River appeared to be slightly slower, clearly losing momentum at the turn, and here there were even some rocks and other flotsam wedged in places that created some eddies. And thirdly, the Riverbanks on both sides appeared to slope at manageable angles.

Success and intuition often go hand in hand.

Vic knew, this was the best place to cross. With that belief, Vic retraced his steps along the bank to where he first encountered the River and then headed back to the Herd.

As Vic approached the Herd, earlier than would have been expected, his approach caused a stir along the ranks. Usually, an early return indicated trouble. Vic was oblivious to this as he was excited that he could now fulfil his task as set by Men-taur.

Word of his approach must have quickly spread through the Herd because there was Men-taur waiting directly ahead of him. "How goes things, Vic?" greeted Men-taur.

Vic responded with a smile, "You knew, Men-taur, didn't you?"

"Knew what?" asked Men-taur innocently.

"You knew I would come across the River at some point?" exclaimed Vic.

"Did I? Imagine having such foresight," replied Men-taur with a smile.

And with that Men-taur and some other leaders he had brought with him proceeded to ask Vic the expected barrage of questions to glean what they needed to prepare the Herd.

Once every last nugget of information had been thoroughly examined, with a few of the leaders heading off in the direction of the River to recce it further, Men-taur motioned for Vic to follow him.

The elders had decided to stop the Herd there for the rest of the day and night with a view to commencing this second Crossing the next day. News spread fast and there was a combination of murmurings to be overheard as Men-taur and Vic weaved their way along the Edge seeking a suitable vantage point to watch the Herd settle in. From there they would be able to look upon the Horizon ahead with a sense of excitement and expectation.

Vic knew that now was the time for the culmination of this lesson — only this time it was different. He really was not sure what the lesson was because Men-taur had not really been with him much since he had been given the scouting responsibility. This time the lesson had not been one event in one day; it had instead arisen over a protracted period of time. In anticipation of the inevitable question, Vic was not completely sure what he had learned.

Men-taur seemed to like knolls, for he chose another one upon which to stop. As always, Vic waited for Men-taur to start. "Okay, Vic, normally, I would ask you to summarize what your lesson has been about. This time, because the lesson has been far more experiential on your part, I suggest we begin by me asking you a series of questions in order to help you glean the learning. How does that sound?" asked Men-taur.

"That sounds good to me, Men-taur. To tell you the truth, I would have found it a challenge to figure out what I had learned just from summarizing my experience as a scout," responded Vic.

"Okay, I understand," acknowledged Men-taur and then added, "Before I begin the questions, I just want to say how proud I am of what you have accomplished and how you have carried out your responsibility as a scout. On behalf of the Herd and the other leaders,

I would like to personally thank you for helping us all get safely to this point in the Journey."

Vic basked briefly in the praise before Men-taur began with the first question, "Okay, Vic, knowing that you were responsible for yourself directly and, the Herd indirectly, what did you have to constantly keep making each day in order to ensure you completed your daily task effectively?"

Vic quietly repeated the question to himself twice; a sudden dawning of awareness came upon him so he replied, "Decisions."

"Indeed, Vic, decisions. And decisions and being Decisive are what this fifth lesson of yours is all about. To be successful and to work toward your Vision, you must be Decisive," exclaimed Men-taur.

Already, Vic's mind was racing to join the dots of all that he had experienced as a scout and all the decisions that he had needed to make for the Herd and for himself.

Lesson 5 - Decisive

"So, Vic, out there beyond your Comfort Zone — or perhaps I should say what used to be your Comfort Zone — where the risk was higher than being within the fold of the Herd, how important was it to be Decisive?" queried Men-taur.

"Very important," promptly replied Vic.

"So, when you were making decisions, were there times when you had to make quick ones?" Men-taur continued.

"Yes, Sir."

"If you had not, what would have happened?" asked Men-taur.

"On one occasion where I had a narrow escape from a Leopard; if I had not acted when I did and in the way in which I did, I may well not have made it back," Vic answered.

"Exactly. So what place was there for indecision?" Men-taur added quickly.

Now the questions seemed to be picking up pace.

"No place," was Vic's short reply.

"So, had you hesitated to make your decision or others like it over your period of scouting, what would have been the outcome?" Men-taur paraphrased his previous question.

"I would not be here," Vic reiterated.

"True," stated Men-taur. "Contrary to popular belief procrastination is not a decision; it can cost you dearly. So, let your 'Yes' be 'Yes' and your 'No' be 'No'," explained Men-taur.

> *Contrary to popular belief procrastination is not a decision; it can cost you dearly.*

Men-taur expanded, "Vic, every day, each Beest or Gazelle must arise with a decision foremost in mind: Each must decide to be ready to run at any given moment; each must decide that each new day it must run faster than the Lion to survive; each day the Lion, equally, must arise and decide to run faster than the Beest or Gazelle to survive. The outcome for both predator and prey is based solely on the decision they each make when they wake up. Of course, they do not know of the obstacles which lay ahead — whether they will be preyed upon or chased that day — but all obstacles can be overcome with the right decisions. So, you have to decide the race you will run each day and the pace you will set. Essentially, your decisions can mean the difference between life and death."

> *...all obstacles can be overcome with the right decisions, So, you have to decide the race you will run each day and the pace you will set.*

As Men-taur allowed Vic to absorb what he was saying, a rhinoceros crossed the plains ahead of them with a calf in tow. The sight prompted Men-taur to add, "Vic, what do you notice about the direction that Rhinoceros and her calf are traveling? Is it a wavering path or a direct one?"

"From here, it looks like a direct one, Men-taur," replied Vic.

"That's right, Vic. Rhinos are short-sighted, and so they move in the direction which is often right in front of them. Now, as you may recall, what was the direction we must keep moving when we are committed to our Vision, and what is the golden rule?" asked Men-taur.

"We are to keep moving forward. We are to, *'Hoof it!'*" answered Vic, and as he did so he also made another connection to the previous lesson about Commitment from when he completed his first Crossing. So he finished his line of thinking out loud, "It is imperative that we keep moving forward and *'Hoof it!'* rather than looking over our shoulder. When I was scouting I realized that if I spent more time looking over my shoulder I would be more concerned with where I had come from than where I was heading. I only needed a brief reference point check on what was behind me because it was more familiar to me. What I needed to pay more attention to was what lay ahead."

"Very well put, Vic," Men-taur agreed. "You must decide if you are intent on being a 'Toward' Beest or an 'Away' Beest. 'Toward' Beest are focused on what lies ahead, and generally invest their energy in the one direction that lies ahead; 'Away' Beest are more intent on grumbling about what they are leaving behind or moving away from, and subsequently spend a lot of energy on not making or being able to make any form of decision. To be a scout or, for that matter, a leader, Vic, which must you be: 'Toward' or 'Away'?" asked Men-taur expectantly.

"A 'Toward'," Vic promptly replied.

"Right! Leaders must be predominantly 'Toward', Vic," Men-taur contributed. "If they are not, then not only will they perish but so will the Herd. 'Toward' leaders are concerned with progress; those with an 'Away' attitude are more concerned with the status quo, regression or stagnation. For both you and me to achieve our own Vision, we must endeavor to remain focused on the Horizon, keep moving forward and *'Hoof it!'*"

Men-taur's questions and explanations had been helping Vic to make some further distinctions as his mind accelerated along the lines of the lesson. A particular thread of thinking was pervading his thoughts, and so he needed to seek clarification. "Men-taur, can I ask you something?" he asked.

"Yes, of course," Men-taur responded encouragingly.

"From my understanding, decisions are forks in our path. 'Yes' takes us down one path and 'No' takes us down another. Effectively, we have a choice to make. To not make a decision keeps us at that fork, and we make no progress and become stuck. Does that sound right?" queried Vic.

"Yes, that's absolutely right," assured Men-taur.

"In that case, to make a comparison, a decision keeps us moving like a flowing River and is continually renewed with life, whereas the inability to make a decision or to instead adopt procrastination is like a stagnant waterhole which has no water flowing into it or out of it; what remains ultimately becomes foul, cannot bear life and becomes a source of illness or even death," concluded Vic.

To that Men-taur summarized, "I would not have thought to put it that way, Vic, but what you say is a great comparison. In short, yes, being Decisive and making decisions keeps you alive to thrive and grow. Actually, your results are determined by your decisions, and who you are at this very moment is determined by the decisions you have made to this point. And, furthermore, who you desire to become will also be determined by your decisions up until now as well as the decisions you have yet to make."

...being Decisive and making decisions keeps you alive to thrive and grow..

In the distance now, they could both see the leaders returning who had gone to investigate the River and the area for the Crossing. Knowing that the time for the lesson was likely drawing to a close, Vic anticipated Men-taur's usual closing question.

"Now is perhaps a good time for me to summarize what I have learned about this lesson regarding decisions and being Decisive and how to apply that learning along my Journey."

Men-taur smiled wryly, uttered a mumbled, "Hhhmmmph" and then just stood waiting for Vic to continue.

With that opening, Vic began, "What is now many days ago, you assigned me with the task of scouting the unknown land ahead of the

Herd and bringing back information on water, grazing and any relevant dangers to the Herd. You actually mentioned at the time that the lesson would become clear when my task was complete. You even mentioned that the rain would have a part to play in the lesson. Today, that lesson concluded with my revelation that the responsibility I assumed as a scout would teach me about making decisions and being Decisive."

Pausing only to order his thoughts rather than gain permission to continue or to check that he was on track, Vic continued, "In my role as scout I had to constantly make decisions. I would come to a point at times where I had a choice to make. Decisions are all about making choices — especially the right ones; the right ones move you forwards while the wrong ones either keep you from progressing or even cause you to go backwards. Indeed, the wrong ones can be costly. Take procrastination as an example. It is not an option nor is it a decision; it leads only to stagnation."

"In order to ensure I was making the best decisions, I had to draw upon my own experience, our previous lessons, and then proceed to ask of myself a series of questions in order to reach the best decision based on the information at hand. The more information I had, the more I could pass on to you, Men-taur, and the other leaders so that you would be fully equipped to make the best decision for the safety and well-being of the Herd."

Vic's lesson recap was now flowing easily. "Regardless of the decision, there is often an associated risk. I learned that risk actually cannot be avoided, like the risk of the next Crossing; risk can only be minimized.

"What I have not shared with you from my experience, Men-taur, is the importance of a heightened awareness when outside my Comfort Zone, and how at times I relied on my intuition to lead me to the right decision."

Men-taur nodded approvingly at this.

"Life is full of choices and therefore decisions," summarized Vic. "My life is determined by my decisions. By always moving forward towards my Vision, paying attention predominantly to what lies ahead rather than what is behind, and making good decisions, I will be able to continue to live and grow."

The leaders were almost back to the Herd now. Vic's summary ended just at the right moment. It was time for another lesson to end. Vic wondered how long he would now have to wait until the next lesson.

As though reading his thoughts, Men-taur added his concluding comments, "Excellent, Vic, excellent. Once again you have tidily summed-up an important lesson and incorporated the other lessons along the way. Your discovery of the power of using your intuition is significant — a true leader learns to use it effectively when making decisions. Vic, you have truly excelled yourself in assuming the role and responsibilities of a scout. You have accounted well for yourself as my student. You have the gratitude of the Herd," Men-taur gave a reassuring smile. "Unlike your previous lessons, Vic, you will not need to wait very long for your next lesson. It begins at dawn. Now, go and get some well-deserved rest. You will need it tomorrow." And, with that, Men-taur headed off in the direction of the returning leaders.

Vic's heart took another excited leap as if to punctuate the conclusion and bedding in of another lesson, as well as the anticipation of the new lesson commencing at the break of dawn. Vic's body, however, finally brought him around and reminded him that he had also not eaten that day. It was time to find some grass and a nice cool drink of fresh rainwater.

"One can choose to go back toward safety or forward toward growth. Growth must be chosen again and again; fear must be overcome again and again."

Maslow

"People begin to become successful the minute they decide to be."

Harvey MacKay

Exercise 5 - Your Being Decisive

As with the previous exercises, please consider this exercise carefully and thoughtfully, as it pertains to successfully achieving your Vision that you noted previously.

1. On a scale of 1-10*, how Decisive are you at making effective and timely decisions to achieve your Vision that you wrote down for Exercise 1? _____

2. In the event that you scored yourself below an 8, what 3 things do you need to be and/or do which will increase your Decisiveness to achieve your Vision to an 8+?

_____

_____

_____

_____

_____

_____

_____

_____

_____

_____

_____

_____

_____

_____

* For this and the other exercises, please note that a score of 1 represents the weakest and a score of 10 represents the strongest.

Chapter Nine

"The door of opportunity won't open unless you do some pushing."

Unknown

"Where you finish in life isn't determined so much by where you start as by whether you start."

Bob Gass

Dawn. A new day and a new lesson. Try as he might, Vic really had not been able to fully rest. He was too excited and energized; excited because of his expectation of another lesson and energized because of his sense of achievement in completing his scouting assignment with Men-taur's praise.

"One good thing about today already is that it's not raining," thought Vic.

That thought brightened him further. The prospect of Crossing in the rain was not one that would fill himself with confidence or the rest of the Herd, for that matter. Vic knew the attitude of the Herd was already at a low ebb and rain would only add a further unhelpful shroud.

Around Vic, the Herd was stirring. The news about the River and the need for this second Crossing had spread at dusk. The news had been received with a mixed response. For some, it was received as good news and, therefore, stirred hope and excitement as those Beest knew — either from previous Journeys or from what they had been told and subsequently believed — that there would be greener grazing on the other side. It also promised a more prolonged rest because this meant they had come near to the completion of another Journey. They had almost made it, and there would soon be the time to slow down, build up body stores, and await the arrival of the new calving season.

For others, however, the news was looked upon from a negative perspective; it was these Beest who were unable to see beyond the Crossing. They did not see it as a route to awaiting rewards; instead, they saw it as a further hardship. To them, this Crossing was looked upon with an unhealthy mix of fear and complaints.

From what Vic had discerned, on the Journey there would always be two Crossings. The Journey followed a circular path and the River bisected that path. From Vic's perspective, the River was not an obstacle; it was exercise — a Crossing only made one stronger.

Breaking free from his thoughts, Vic raised himself from his prone observations and contemplations. He took some time to stretch, slake his thirst from a nearby puddle, and graze what little pickings of grass were nearby.

The sun was already shining through the trees which lined the River in the distance. The air was heavy from the humidity and added to the heat burden. Flies thronged in annoying clouds. The resultant prevailing sound from every direction was the irritated swishing of tails.

With only a whisper of wind caressing his face, Vic set out. As he knew the Crossing would take the good part of the day and that Men-taur would be overseeing preparations, Vic decided to take the initiative and seek out Men-taur early, and so he headed towards the River.

Shortly, Vic was beyond the Edge and, with that transition, his senses re-tuned to the customary alertness which he had developed as a scout and was ultimately able to switch on when required. Along the way, he passed the odd Beest heading back to the Herd, likely to pass on instructions. When he did, he could not help but utter a lively, "Good Morning!"

As far as Vic was concerned, this would be a great day; he felt optimistic about the Crossing, his lesson and his Vision.

Once he reached the line of trees, Vic turned and retraced his steps from the day before. As he negotiated around a cluster of bushes, he almost bumped into Men-taur who was heading his way with another leader. With no evidence of surprise, Men-taur simply greeted, "Good morning, Vic."

"Good morning, Men-taur!" Vic replied with a double nod to include the other leader, who also nodded in return.

They all came to a stop, facing each other. As always, Vic waited for Men-taur to continue. In the interim, Men-taur had turned slightly to give the other Beest some final instructions. After a few moments, the other Beest headed away, nodding his head respectfully towards Men-taur and added a further, perhaps surprising nod, in Vic's direction. Men-taur looked at Vic and paused.

What would have been a silent pause between them out on the plains was now a tremoring pause here. The rushing River announced its presence through the vibrating air; its power was palpable despite the fact that it could not be seen from where they stood.

"Walk with me, Vic," directed Men-taur.

Men-taur began to head in the direction from which Vic had just come, and so Vic had to turn around. "I was just coming to see you," Men-taur began. "I was not expecting to bump into you out here. I was expecting to have to wake you up," he added with a straight face but with a smiling twinkle in his eye.

Vic did not hide his smile. "I awoke excited about today and knew that you would be busy with the Crossing so I thought I would come and find you to save you some time."

"Thank you for your thoughtful initiative," Men-taur acknowledged and then continued unabated, "As you are already out here, let's head to one of the staging areas or Waiting Zones, as you call them, to set you onto your new lesson."

Vic's mouth hung open and his eyes had widened in surprise.

"Seeing the surprised expression on your face is a treat, Vic....Yes, we took your suggestions for improving a Crossing and have created not one Waiting Zone but a series of them. We leaders thought having more than one would increase the safety factor and establish greater control for the Crossing. Once we developed your idea, all involved could see the logic of it. Subsequently, everyone wanted me to relay to you his or her thanks."

Vic once again felt that flushing in his face, and did not know really where to look, still finding praise uncomfortable at times. Remembering his manners, Vic added a humble, "You're welcome."

Shortly, they arrived at the staging area. The only reason Vic knew they had arrived was because Men-taur stopped. The area was unremarkable aside from a nearby pile of dung that, admittedly, seemed more than one Beest could be responsible for.

As often happened, Men-taur seemed to sense his question. "Now, how would you know this was a staging area?" Men-taur asked rhetorically, because he then answered, "Because, each one is marked by a pile of dung similar to what you see there. A new innovation. Admittedly, as you anticipated, Vic, we do not have much time before we gather in the Herd and get started with the Crossing. With that in mind, please just give me a brief summary of your lesson on decisions and being Decisive. While I know that the lesson is very fresh in your mind, it is nevertheless always important to review what you have learned. When you do so, you are reinforcing the lesson. Once you have completed that, we will move on to the task at hand — the Crossing — and your next lesson. Okay?"

"Yes. Okay, Men-taur," agreed Vic with a nod.

Knowing that these sessions followed a now familiar pattern, Vic no longer waited to be asked to begin. He just did. "As you just mentioned, the lesson was concerned with decisions and being Decisive. A successful leader must be Decisive and be able to consistently make good decisions — not only for him or her, but also for those who are following. Unlike previous lessons, most of my learning on this occasion took place away from you. The lesson required that I take responsibility for the assigned task of scouting ahead to help the Herd establish a safe route through an unknown area which would also simultaneously meet the water and grazing needs.

"Out beyond the Edge, I had to gather information about the area ahead and make decisions for both myself and the Herd, which had to be done in an almost moment-by-moment fashion so that I could fulfil my assignment adequately and effectively. Because it was often down to me, I had to be decisive, especially at times of imminent danger.

"Making decisions arises when I have a choice. When I make the right decision it moves me forwards; the wrong one will either lead me backwards or at best keep me at the fork in the path of choices. Contrary to what many Beest and other animals believe, to not make a decision or to procrastinate is not a decision and could prove to be very costly to both myself and the Herd. Often, in order to reach an effective decision, I am required to ask myself a series of questions relative to my experience and the information which has been gathered. This is also the time when I need to listen to my own intuition. Almost every decision I make carries with it some risk or consequence; such risk can only be minimized and rarely avoided. Finally," indicated Vic, "my life and the results I achieve are determined by my decisions. Being Decisive and making good decisions means that I will continue to grow throughout my life."

"Thank you, Vic. Brief and comprehensive," said Men-taur appreciatively.

The sun had now climbed over the trees as a glowing ball of oppressive heat, and there was now no shelter that could shield its intensity — at least not from where they stood. Both Vic and Men-taur had sheens of sweat along their flanks and necks beginning to glisten in the light. While it was meant to help cool them down, it had a seemingly magnetic affect on the flies; neither the heat nor the sweat seemed to deter them. Instead, they continued their pursuit of annoying bother, biting and flying tactics. The result was an ascending frequency with which the two Beest's tails and ears twitched.

Snorting a small posse of flies from the end of his black moistened muzzle, Men-taur broke the interlude. "Okay, this Crossing will be the source of your next lesson. As with your last one, you will likely discover the object of this lesson once the Crossing is over and the Herd is safely on the other side of the River. Since you discharged yourself so admirably as a scout, it is time, I believe, to give you an increased level of responsibility. This is the next progressive step in your lessons and your own development."

Men-taur gave Vic some time for this to sink in before continuing. At the same time he looked toward the direction of the Herd and noted that the Herd was now moving fully towards them. "Okay Vic," Men-taur began whilst indicating with a tilt of his head in the direction of the Herd, "time marches on and so must the Herd."

"As you can likely see, while there is plenty of water around us thanks to all the rain, what is lacking here is sufficient grass to sustain the Herd. The Herd is already tired due to our detour around Man, which has significantly lengthened our Journey. Morale and resources are waning, Vic; this means that the Crossing must happen today. Based on the pattern of rain which I have been recently observing on our Horizon, I know from experience that what we will find on the other side of the River will be the Herd's reward — rest and replenishment. And so, the sooner we get the Herd across the River, the happier every Beest will be."

Now that the preamble was over, Men-taur got straight to Vic's new lesson responsibility. "Okay, Vic, you made three suggestions after the last Crossing. We have already discussed the implementation of Waiting Zones. What were the other two?" questioned Men-taur.

Vic's response was immediate. He had reviewed his lessons on a daily basis to ensure they were remembered and integrated into who he was becoming. "One was creating a buddy system for all calves and injured or weakened Beest, so that when the time comes for crossing the River, the buddy will cross beside them on the upstream side to reduce some of the effort for them to cross. The last suggestion was setting up rescue teams composed of strong swimmers to help those who are struggling to cross or who are stranded on this side of the River due to injury, fear or weakness."

"Right!" agreed Men-taur. "Each of these recommendations is now in place, Vic. What I would now like you to do is two-fold. First, you will oversee this Waiting Zone. There will be a leader here as support. Use their support as you require. Your group will be the first one we will call forward to Cross. Part of your responsibility will be to provide instructions and to assign the buddies and also make sure that no Beest leaves the Zone until signaled forward with the others within this Zone. I will leave it to your judgement to determine how to do that. The second part of your responsibility is to coordinate the rescue teams on the far bank. The rescue teams will operate as required between each group Crossing, as well as to bring over the last few stragglers after the final group has crossed. Is that clear, Vic?" Men-taur asked.

"Yes," answered Vic, then confirmed, "First, I am to oversee and control this Waiting Zone, assigning buddies according to my judgement and, second, once I am across, I am to coordinate the rescue teams from the far bank in order to help bring in the stragglers and stranded."

"Good. Good," Men-taur agreed.

A large group of Beest were now noisily approaching.

"Well, Vic, the time has come for me to head over to the River. As you can see now, your group is just arriving. I will likely see you briefly before you cross. I will not be Crossing with you. Be safe."

As Men-taur quickly headed off towards the River, Vic was registering the impact of Men-taur's last statement — he was not going to be with him during his Crossing. Vic felt his confidence and excitement begin to wane; he had wrongly assumed that Men-taur would be his own buddy.

As the group leader approached, Vic quietly and quickly remonstrated himself. A panoramic flash of memory showed him just what he had endured on this Journey and through the lessons he had learned. Suddenly, he became aware of how much Men-taur must believe in him to assign him with the responsibility he had just been given.

The leader was a big bull — or would have been had Vic not grown so much recently. Vic realized that whilst he still might need some depth and width to his chest, he was nearly as tall as this bull — and that was just the additional boost Vic had needed to turn the tide of his confidence.

Vic was as ready as he would ever be. Now, it was time to turn his attention to the needs of others rather than himself. He had some responsibilities to fulfil.

The bull came up to Vic and just nodded and offered up a gruff, "Morning".

Following courtesy, Vic nodded and returned the greeting in a similar fashion. "Good morning." Vic then waited on the bull respectfully. Nothing was forthcoming until the entire group had arrived at the Waiting Zone.

With a hint of contempt the bull spoke, "The name's Dow-taur. Men-taur has told me that you are to give us the Crossing instructions, including assigning the buddies. He also informed me that you will be co-ordinating the first rescue team once we get to the other side."

With some initial hesitation brought on by the dour and, even, questioning nature of the bull, Vic replied, "Yes, Dow-taur, that's correct; that's what Men-taur just instructed me on before he left."

"Well," said Dow-taur impatiently, "you had better get on with it. Men-taur seems to have been impressed by you. Now's the time to prove your mettle."

"Uh… Yes, of course, Dow-taur," Vic said, somewhat troubled. He had not expected to be confronted and challenged before he even got started in his new assignment.

Vic decided to look beyond this challenge and remind himself of the faith Men-taur had put in him. He had to act. He held that thought as he turned more squarely to instruct the group which had gathered. It was a big group; larger than he had expected. He certainly could not see to the back of the group. The weight of just this part of the responsibility was dawning upon him, and his stomachs responded by starting to churn.

The group turned toward Dow-taur expecting him to speak. When he didn't, the Beest closest to the front looked confused as they saw him looking towards Vic, which subsequently caused Vic's stomachs to churn that little bit more.

Feeling a rising tide of panic, Vic checked himself, incanted to himself, *"Hoof it!"* as he took several slow deep breaths. Lifting his head, Vic then began as he meant to finish – with purpose and intent.

"GOOD MORNING!" Vic shouted as loud as he thought required to reach the entire group. A few Beest along the front looked at each

other and then back at Vic. "GOOD MORNING!" Vic shouted even
louder still. A few more heads turned from the anxious rumbling that
seemed to emanate from within the group.

Dow-taur became impatient. "PAY ATTENTION!" boomed
Dow-taur who then turned his attention exaggeratedly toward Vic.
The rumbling stopped.

"THANK YOU DOW-TAUR," Vic shouted respectfully in reply,
however, realizing that his volume no longer required to be so loud,
he dropped his voice down to a more manageable level. "Men-taur
and Dow-taur have delegated responsibility to me to provide you with
instructions concerning today's Crossing," Vic began.

Vic registered that by including Dow-taur with Men-taur in his
opening, Dow-taur's countenance both softened towards him and
swelled with his own importance. Wishing to acknowledge and respect
especially the other adult Beest, Vic continued, "As you will have
determined for yourselves already, this Crossing will be unlike any
previous ones. As you will also realize, we have had to face some other
changes to our Journey. The leadership have made these changes in
order to make your Journey as safe as possible and to reach the end
of the Journey with as many of our Herd in safety. These changes have
been applied as they are seen as inevitable when striving to ensure
progress, and are for each of our own benefit as well as that of the
Herd as a whole."

There was a mixture of nodding and the shaking of heads.

"As you all will recall from the last Crossing, when we began there
was a surging forward and, because there was only so much space in
the bank to get down to the River, the press of Beest led to panic and,
sadly, made the Crossing very dangerous, which concluded with some
of our own becoming either trampled or injured. How many of you can
remember how that felt?"

Vic paused to ensure he was being understood. He noted from the
Beest nearest that he could see that all were nodding. His empathy
worked because, from then on, he had the group's attention.

"As with the last Crossing there is only limited access which has been deemed safe enough to cross. To minimize panic and the danger this situation brings, the leaders, such as Dow-taur, have decided it is therefore best for the Herd to cross in these smaller groups as opposed to one big Herd. Once each group has crossed safely, the next group will then be called forward to the River's edge. Is that understood?"

Vic realized it was important to check understanding as he progressed with the instructions to ensure that every Beest understood.

"This group has the honor of going first. I will support Dow-taur to bring us all down to the River's edge. Dow-taur will give the signal and lead us all across safely."

Dow-taur began to nod in agreement and stamped the ground proudly. He was relishing the added attention. As far as Vic was concerned, Dow-taur was more interested in his own importance than the safety of the group.

Seeing that the Beest remained focused on him, Vic continued. "Another initiative from the leadership for every Beest's safety is the implementation of a buddy system. Again, as I am sure you will recall from the last Crossing, the uncontrolled press and panic combined with the force of the River caused some Beest — particularly the calves, injured and elderly — to not make it across. You may even have personally known some of them."

Again, a sea of sad nods rippled through the groups.

"For today's Crossing, we will be establishing a buddy system to ensure that every orphaned calf, injured or elderly Beest is paired up with an adult or strong yearling who will be able to aid them during the Crossing. And, with the objective of further ensuring the safety of each of you, the responsible adult or yearling must swim on the upstream side of their buddy. This will provide an added measure of protection and safety from the River's full force. Do you all understand?"

While at the front there were nods, Vic could not be sure that those at the back understood. Rather than continue with the rest of the briefing, Vic needed to establish that everyone understood the last instruction, and so he walked over to Dow-taur and asked how to best approach this.

Appreciating the courtesy and the foresight, Dow-taur agreed that understanding was important; after all, he did not wish to appear a fool as his group had the honor of going first.

After some discussion, they agreed that the best thing to do was to break the group into even smaller groups. Those adults who had been at the front of the group and had been listening to the instructions were delegated with the responsibility of relaying understanding to an assigned group. And, once it was established they had all understood the instructions, they were then requested to allocate buddies as required.

Vic, joined by Dow-taur, moved amongst the smaller groups in no particular order to further reinforce the instructions. Vic was surprised by the initial resistance to the changes. But, with some further clarification and justification of the new Crossing procedures along with the answering of any questions, the group slowly became reassured about the increased safety the methods would provide.

Vic and Dow-taur had decided during the initial discussion to separately pass on the additional instructions pertaining to the rescue teams. Within each group they identified who had the size, strength and experience required to be potentially called upon should the need arise for them to help with stragglers or those who may have been lost or have otherwise become separated from their buddy. With Dow-taur looking on, Vic asked each Beest identified to join with them once they reached the opposite bank, and advised that they could then coordinate from there.

Once each sub-group had been briefed and understanding had been confirmed, Vic headed back to the front of their Waiting Zone. As he approached the front, Vic could now see that some groups had since arrived at a designated area and others were still on their way from where the main Herd had bedded down for the night.

Men-taur was at the front when he got there.

"Is your group ready?" Men-taur asked simply, nodding to Dow-taur who was emerging from amidst the two foremost sub-groups.

"Yes, Men-taur," Vic replied simply.

"Okay then, it is time to get started," directed Men-taur, "the River is not going to wait and neither can we. There have been distant rumblings of thunder upstream foretelling of more rain, which could make the Crossing more treacherous as the day wears on."

Vic nodded in understanding.

"I will join you and Dow-taur down to the River's bank," Men-taur stated and then turned.

Vic turned to face the group and simply ordered, "Follow me." Seeing the group begin to move in his direction, Vic caught up with Men-taur to flank him on his nearside as Dow-taur was on the other.

No more words were spoken until they all reached the riverbank. The River's roar did not appear to have lessened. As they approached, Vic could immediately sense the tension in the group behind due to the increase in intensity of nervous murmuring.

Men-taur led them to the lip of the riverbank. Signaling to stop, Men-taur found a small raised mound just off to the side where he could be seen and from where his voice would be carried across the group. Then, he motioned for Vic and Dow-taur to join him. Once all three of them were facing the group, Men-taur looked at Vic and tilted his head in the direction of the group. Vic realized he was meant to address them.

His stomachs began to churn so, taking a deep breath, Vic shouted, "MY FELLOW BEEST. THE TIME HAS COME FOR THE SECOND CROSSING ON THIS JOURNEY. WE HAVE THE HONOR OF BEING THE FIRST GROUP TO CROSS USING THE NEW PROCEDURES. WE WILL ENDEAVOR TO SET THE EXAMPLE FOR THE REST OF THE HERD." Vic paused to breathe then, recalling his lesson from his first Crossing, added, "IT IS TIME FOR ACTION. REMEMBER — FOCUS ON THE OTHER SIDE, COMMIT TO YOURSELF AND TO YOUR BUDDY AND YOU WILL MAKE IT. IT IS TIME TO 'HOOF IT!'"

Some Beest in the group felt inspired enough to bellow in support and the rest of the group soon joined in. Vic smiled in return.

Men-taur's eyes danced as he lowered his muzzle towards the group. Vic took that as a signal for him to return to the group.

Vic returned to the group and now sought out his buddy. Due to his size, he had been assigned to buddy with an elderly cow called Elle-taur. She greeted him with an encouraging grin. Dow-taur paired up with his buddy.

"AWAIT THE SIGNAL," Men-taur boomed.

As with the last time, a brief hush followed. Every Beest knew that this Crossing truly led to greener pastures, and to cross required not only intention and commitment but also purposeful action.

From where Vic was positioned he could see the River surging by, carrying with it flotsam of various size. It was churning almost angrily in places; in a few places upstream and downstream from this vantage point there were islands of twisted logs and branches stuck against some rocks. Occasionally, a log would break free and be tossed about once it hit the full onslaught of the main stream. Vic was sure the River was wilder than that of the last Crossing.

A mixture of anxiety and excitement battled within Vic. He knew he had to channel all of his focus and energy into getting not only himself but also Elle-taur to the other side. To help him bolster his courage, he looked over at Elle-taur already positioned on what would be his downstream side. He smiled encouragingly.

Elle-taur smiled perceptively in return and then quietly whispered in his ear, "You cannot control the River but you can control how you approach it and how you respond to it. You either control your environment or it controls you."

You either control your environment or it controls you.

Vic widened his eyes and his smile beamed. Elle-taur's advice boosted his resolve and fired his courage. And so, despite his anxiety and fear, Vic realized that true courage is a willingness to take action irrespective of fears.

...true courage is a willingness to take action
irrespective of fears.

"Thank you Elle-taur, let's both *'Hoof it!'*" Vic whispered emphatically back.

Elle-taur smiled. Clearly, she had done many Journeys. She knew the Way of Things and accepted them.

Vic swelled with further Commitment to get Elle-taur to the other side.

Around them a calm tension had come over the group and, with it, a quiet resolve of absolute Commitment descended; Vic could sense it from the furrowed brows and the leveled horns pointing threateningly towards the water as if it were a foe to be confronted head-on. Conversations had ceased. This time, he noticed that there was room to breathe as there was no press of bodies crammed in this approach gauntlet as there had been with his first Crossing. At the other end of the gauntlet was survival.

Just then, a booming bellow reverberated around the group and, for a moment, drowned out the River. Unlike before when a lone bull tested the River first, it was deemed prudent to let that be a practice of the past. As one the group now lunged forward knowing that momentum was required to enter the River — now was not the time to waste time.

From those observing from a distance, it suddenly appeared that within mere seconds the Earth had swallowed up the entire group.

Dow-taur led the charge. The front ranks hit the water — a stoppable force meeting an unstoppable one. Nature versus nature. The River churned by in seeming disregard for the Beest.

The buddy system kicked in with bellows of encouragement and shouts of *"HOOF IT!"* Those who were first to hit the water were now lunging into the mainstream and, with that, many seemed to disappear as the bottom fell away from under them. It was time to swim, and time to use the current to help to get to the other side.

Because of the size of the group and the buddy system, every Beest reached the water — this time, none had been trampled.

Vic would notice this later because both he and Elle-taur were in the second rank. Both hit the water. Both felt the cold crush shock their systems, speed up their breathing and lash at their faces. Vic fixed his eyes on a particular tree on the opposite bank and the place immediately beneath it where he intended to land along with Elle-taur. Vic was now fueled by his Vision, Commitment, Passion and responsibility.

"I'm with you, Elle-taur," gasped Vic, as he lunged forward further into the River and its onslaught and received a welcoming mouthful of water.

Because his body was taking the brunt of the River's impact, he was swept into Elle-taur. Both of them began churning their legs, while the River angrily tore at them, disrupting any likelihood of true rhythm.

Before fully succumbing to the effort of the Crossing, Vic glimpsed both ahead and immediately around him and could see that there appeared to be several two-headed Beest thrashing against the water. With that awareness, Vic registered that, so far, the buddy system was working.

And then, suddenly, the bottom dropped from beneath Vic's feet. Briefly, he went under but quickly came back up gasping and spluttering. Nevertheless, his focus still remained on the opposite bank; yes, his heart may have raced up a notch but he knew it was time to swim for all he was worth. Now was not the time for words, but for action. Elle-taur was still by his side and, although their legs threatened to get tangled, both of them kept going.

Now they were in midstream and the force of the flow was propelling them and others downstream despite their best efforts. Vic felt Elle-taur begin to slip further downstream. He knew he had to stick close by. Despite his head only just being above the surface of the water, he managed to shout to her.

"I'M COMING!"

He angled himself so he was carried a bit more in her direction. Within moments he was by her side again but she was clearly in distress with the whites of her eyes showing, nostrils flared and snorting nearly at double the speed of Vic's. He realized that if he did not act quickly, this Journey could be Elle-taur's last.

Vic took in Elle-taur's predicament and made a fast decision. He quickly slipped back behind her and then swam alongside her on the down-stream side. Whilst she was taking the impact of the River, he was ultimately in a better position to support her and push her towards the opposite side.

Immediately, as he did so, Vic realized just what he had committed himself to. Vic's effort to swim increased as Elle-taur's rapidly weakening state meant she was contributing less to their progress.

"Hang on!" Vic snorted, gritting his teeth. "Just... keep ... moving ... forward!" he accentuated with successive breaths.

Elle-taur's legs moved more in reflex than in any great coordinated effort. She was in trouble, and Vic knew that if he wasn't careful, they both would be — and that would require a difficult decision.

Just then, Vic felt something under a hoof. His leg seemed to recognize the solid riverbed because it signaled a renewed effort to the rest of his body. Within moments his other hooves were in regular contact with the bottom. Elle-taur was sagging beside him. Now, with his head and chest beginning to clear the water and his legs churning beneath him, he was able to more forcefully support Elle-taur with his head lowered against her side. He pushed with his hind legs, which seemed to jolt Elle-taur as she found a final reserve of energy. With a final push they lunged for the nearby bank.

They had made it!

They were one of the last pairings of the rank to reach the bank. Elle-taur nearly collapsed once away from the River's edge. Both of them had steam rising from their bodies – a mixture of cold water and hot sweat. Their muscles quivered and trembled beneath their skin.

"Hang on, Elle-taur," Vic said encouragingly, "let's get you safely up the bank".

Elle-taur only grunted in response.

The River had physically taken its toll. Around them were a few other Beest who were now weakly struggling up the bank. Vic looked around more widely and noted that they appeared not to have lost any Beest — a great result, but nevertheless one which he could not focus on as he was intent on getting Elle-taur safely up the bank.

With some nudging and shoving, he managed to half encourage and half push Elle-taur up the bank. Finally, they crested its top. All seemed clear. Already off to one side there appeared to be several Beest together in what could only be deemed a recovery area. Most were the elderly, young or lame. Vic directed Elle-taur in that direction. Once there, she sank to the ground with exhaustion. She was breathing heavily but the fear had gone from her eyes. Her eyes spoke volumes of thanks while she could only mouth an exhausted, "Thank you."

Aware of his ongoing responsibilities, Vic knew he had to quickly get back down to the River. "Elle-taur, you rest here until you feel stronger. You did so well. Please excuse me, I need to get back to my duties."

Elle-taur managed a nod and a tilt of her head as if she were discharging him from her service. Vic reluctantly turned back towards the River and headed down the bank. Dow-taur was there waiting for him off to one side. All the other Beest selected as potential rescuers were either with Dow-taur or heading in that direction.

As he approached, Dow-taur simply noted, "I see you made it."

"Yes, Dow-taur. Thank you."

Dow-taur then asked, "So, should we now call for the next group to cross?"

"Not yet, I think Dow-taur," Vic replied, "Let's just remind everyone of what we are meant to do, because all this is new and all of us have just battled a Crossing. It would be good for us to be prepared first."

"Makes sense I suppose," Dow-taur agreed. Looking around at the bedraggled group, he spoke up for all to hear. "Gather round, all. It is now time to go over what we need to do next." Dow-taur then nodded in Vic's direction, dictating that he was passing the responsibility to him.

"Okay, everyone," Vic began inclusively, "let's just review the briefing to ensure we know what we are supposed to do. As we have just crossed, if you have any useful ideas or feedback that will help us to help the rest of the Herd cross, please let us know."

Vic paused and then, hearing no response, he continued, "Our role is to provide support on this side for the next group that crosses.

That support can take on several forms from shouting encouragement to helping weakened Beest ashore and up to the recovery area. Also we can help to reunite separated family members and, hopefully, only exceptionally, have to cross again to the other side to buddy and rescue the stranded, weakened and afraid. The latter will actually only take place once the last group has crossed. We are responsible for this for the remainder of the Crossing. This is because we will be the most recovered to be able to face a further double Crossing. Does everyone understand?"

Vic was greeted by a ring of nods. Seeing this response he added, "Are there any questions or comments?"

One young bull spoke up, "Yes, what happens if we get tired?"

"A good question," Vic replied, "In the event you are called into action before the final Crossing and feel too tired to go on, please let either Dow-taur or myself know. We will then replace you with nominated rescuers from the ensuing groups. Any more questions?" Vic asked.

None were forthcoming.

"Okay. Now, let's call over that we are ready for the next group. To be best prepared, let's split ourselves in half: One group take the upstream side of the Crossing point, and the other take the downstream side."

Vic took half to the downstream side, while Dow-taur and his group took the upstream side. Once both teams were in place, Dow-taur let out a bellow signaling for the next group.

The next group quickly poured over the lip of the opposite bank in a brown and gray wave. Vic noted more objectively that the buddy system was clearly evident as the group charged toward the water. As the group hit the water, he and the others began to shout encouragement. They chanted, "Hoof it!" as enthusiastically as they dared considering they also needed to conserve their own energy in the event that they needed to go into action.

With this second group, there were a few occasions where one of the team stepped in to support those struggling, helping them to make it ashore. Vic, himself, waded out into the shallower water along the River's edge to help push a weaker Beest ashore. Vic would then direct one of the team to see that they made it up to the recovery area on top of the bank where he had left Elle-taur.

Vic reassuringly noticed that not one Beest had been trampled on the other side. He also noticed a regrettable few Beest who hadn't made it across; one or two had managed to struggle back to the opposite shore, while a few others were carried away by the River, never to be seen again. At such a time, Vic and the team had to make a decision — were they to attempt a rescue or let Nature run its course.

In fact, Vic and another Beest did try to rescue a couple of times and barely made it back to the bank with their own lives — the River was just too strong. Though the loss and inevitability of it weighed upon Vic heavily, he nevertheless reminded himself that only the fit survive — a grim reminder that it was the Way of Things.

Time marched on. The River surged by. Further groups crossed. Most survived. Some didn't. Vic and his team were kept busy. As the Crossing progressed, they had to replace some of the original rescuers due to fatigue.

Finally, it got to the point in the Crossing where there was only one group left to come across. Vic had not seen Men-taur as yet, and so he assumed he would be in this last group. Vic signaled across to Dow-taur to call the final group across.

Dow-taur's bellow still hung on the air as the final group charged over the rim and down to the River. From Vic's viewpoint, it all now seemed routine — an almost life-and-death routine.

Vic could not make out Men-taur as the group hit the water, but Vic had to opt to abandon his hopeful search as he and his team went into action shouting encouragement.

Before long, Vic found himself back in the water helping a young bull push a struggling old bull out of the water. The young bull appeared exhausted, and so Vic offered to take over with getting the old bull up to the recovery area.

Taking over required more effort than he had originally expected: The bull was far bigger than Elle-taur had been but, fortunately, halfway up the bank, the old bull's pride kicked in. He shook off Vic's assistance and managed the rest of the way himself.

Vic turned back. As he did so, his eyes caught sight of Men-taur emerging from the River with his buddy. Vic felt both elated and relieved. He walked down the bank tentatively due to all the mud that now slicked the slope from all the dripping water and churning from the passing Beest. As Vic approached Men-taur with a mirrored smile, he noted that the last few Beest were entering the River to complete this Crossing. It was a welcome sight for Vic; it had been a long and tiring day. Seeing Men-taur gave him a boost of energy that sped around his body.

"Hello, Vic," Men-taur panted. No more words were forthcoming as Men-taur needed a few moments at least to recover from his Crossing.

"Hello, Men-taur," Vic replied.

Men-taur did not move, nor did he say anything further as he gathered his breath. Vic waited respectfully. As he did so he kept a watchful eye on the final few Beest as they came across the River. Dow-taur was also watching from his vantage point upstream. There were a few other rescuers with him. Vic's group were in place with a similar vigilance.

Suddenly, Vic heard rather than saw, a paired bawling cry from the River. Quickly, he scanned the water's surface; two Beest were lunging desperately. They were not making progress. And then, when chaos was already apparent, a long leathery tail broke the surface and thrashed the water nearby. A Crocodile. A large head emerged and instantly clamped onto the hind leg of one of the struggling Beest. When it seemed like things couldn't get worse, another Crocodile also emerged close to the other Beest. The Beests' panic increased.

Before any rescuer — or other Beest, for that matter — could react in any way, a violent ominous slap of the Crocodiles' tails could be heard as they quickly dragged both Beest back into deeper water and dragged them underwater. They never resurfaced.

"I'm sorry, you had to witness that event, Vic," Men-taur said regretfully as he came up behind Vic. "I thought we had managed to escape the Crocodiles this time. They are always a threat to the Crossing. And, while I am saddened by our loss, I must remind myself that from what I have observed today, this has been the most successful Crossing ever."

Vic scarcely listened to what Men-taur had to say. He felt more than regret; he somehow felt responsible for the loss. His mind was racing to determine what he could have done to save those Beest.

Noting Vic's inner turmoil, Men-taur opted to supportively stand by. This was something that Vic was going to have to deal with and, no doubt, for every Journey of the future. But, with every incident comes a lesson, and Men-taur was sure that the learning from this traumatic event would only strengthen his young protégé.

The last Beest struggled ashore, wide-eyed after having quickened their efforts to cross. Witnessing the Crocodiles' lethal attack at close quarters had added an urgent motivation to get out of the water.

Dow-taur was heading over with one other rescuer, having apparently discharged the rest. "Our job is done, although it's a shame about those two," Dow-taur commented as he approached. He nodded in Men-taur's direction.

Before Men-taur could reply, Vic broke out of his bruising self-analysis and exclaimed, "Our job is not done, Dow-taur. We must fulfil our final responsibility, to get the last stragglers across. As you can surely see," Vic tossed his head towards the opposite bank, "there are a few Beest over there, and they need our help."

Sure enough, there were several Beest bawling in distress on the other side running to and fro along the riverbank; whether they were disoriented, afraid, weakened — or a combination all of these — Vic and the others could not tell. Nevertheless, Vic felt compelled into action. Aware that the Crocodiles might return soon, Vic knew that the sooner they attempted to help the stranded stragglers, the safer the subsequent Crossings would be.

Without really consulting Men-taur or Dow-taur, Vic sprung into action. One prevalent thought resonated in his head. "I must finish my duties." Reflexively, he called over his team of rescuers who were still at their posts. He split them into two unequal groups: One group would join him to cross back over to gather the stragglers together and, once on the other side, each rescuer would be assigned to buddy up with a straggler; the second group would stay on this side, maintain watch, and support as required when the first group returned with their charges.

Vic looked briefly over his shoulder towards Men-taur; he could not fully read Men-taur's face but he sensed Men-taur's encouragement by the way he was standing square and tall, almost as though he was part of the ground, as though he was immovable. Vic knew his brief and Men-taur knew it. Men-taur had a responsibility for the safety of the entire Herd. He would not be joining Vic.

Dow-taur just stood expressionless next to Men-taur.

Vic turned, flanked by his rescuers, and charged into the River yelling, *"HOOF IT!"*Once again, Vic kept his focus on the opposite bank. He was so fired up that he barely noticed the cold dragging force of the water. He reached out with his legs for the water beneath and around him and propelled it behind him.

Somehow, Vic made it to the other side without a full recall of just how. Surprisingly, rather than feeling fatigued despite all of his efforts of the day, Vic felt in full control: His decisions were his to make and his action were his to take.

Around him, the other rescuers were climbing out of the water. As they did, some of the stragglers were greeting them, pleading for help. Still, others ran up the bank and disappeared over the top.

Vic and his team gathered the stragglers at the River's edge and headed up the bank. They knew they would have to gather in the others at the top. Vic also knew they would need the momentum of the charge back down the bank to help the stragglers overcome any fear or hesitation. Hopefully, they could create a small stampede where each Beest would be caught up in its own momentum and follow the Beest in front without being fully aware of why or where they were heading.

Time was pressing; the Crossing had already consumed most of the day. The sun was now setting and the trees and the steep bank were beginning to cast long shadows. A night Crossing was far too dangerous and was not an option.

With urgency, Vic sent out the rescuers to round up every Beest they could find. Vic and another rescuer kept watch over stragglers nearby who were clinging to them as a newborn calf would to its mother.

Finally, all the rescuers returned with the last few Beest. One reported that he had heard Lion nearby, and Vic realized that, once again, it was time to act. In addition, Vic also realized that there were slightly more stragglers than rescuers, which ultimately posed a challenge — he would not be able to buddy-up every Beest.

Vic's mind raced to come up with a solution. In what was now developing into an emergency, Vic concluded that time is life. He looked around at his team and simply asked, "Ideas?"

A few of the team had noticed the dilemma but only shook their heads. One suggested that they should just take the youngest and strongest back.

...time is life.

But, this was not an option Vic wanted to consider. Then an idea came to him.

"Okay!" Vic began firmly, "Listen up. All of you who have not yet managed to Cross today, will cross with us. We are here to help you. To ensure your safety, my team and I will buddy-up with you as best as we can. However, your numbers are more than ours. If you now feel strong enough with us here to assume a buddy role, let me know now. The rest of you will cross between us. Some of us will flank you as support as we cross on the downstream side and the others will provide upstream protection and support. Is that understood?"

The response was a series of nods of varying intensity.

Just then, a Lion roared nearby. A few Beest spooked, broke ranks and fled. One of the rescuers made to follow.

"HOLD!" Vic shouted. The rescuer stopped mid-stride.

"We do not have time nor can we now run the risk of further losses," Vic emphasized. "We will have to let them go. Sometimes, we have to sacrifice the few for the good of the many."

A Lion roared again. Closer, this time.

Sometimes, we have to sacrifice the few
for the good of the many.

It was time to move. Vic moved purposefully to the left rear flank of the group. As he did so, he shouted, "REMEMBER, STICK CLOSE, FOCUS ON THE OTHER SIDE AND *'HOOF IT!'"*

As the final rescuer assumed his position, Vic let out an almighty bellow. Every Beest launched into action. By the time the group crested the bank they were all at a canter. The slope of the bank added to the momentum. Each Beest hit the water at a gallop.

As Vic was at the back, he noted that every remaining straggler was still with them. The mini stampede idea had worked, and had likely been spurred on by the idea of the Lion behind them.

The shadows of the approaching dusk had not yet reached the opposite bank. As he fixed his eyes on the same tree as before, Vic noted that Men-taur still stood in the spot where Vic had left him.

Then, Vic's thoughts were diverted as he became consumed by the task at hand as he hit the water. A young cow was next to him. Together, they lunged forwards until the water deepened. The chilling water caught Vic's breath as his hooves suddenly found only water. The cow's body was swept into Vic's. Vic snorted some staccato encouragement, "Hoof... it!... You... will... make...it." No reply was forthcoming, nor was one expected.

From where Men-taur stood, the group was doing well. Whether it was due to fear, determination or some other factor, the entire group seemed to be traversing the River quickly.

Movement downstream caught Men-taur's eye. Where the shadow crossed by the light of the remaining sun, Men-taur made out the clear outline of another Crocodile. Whether it was one of the ones which had attacked before, Men-taur did not know. This time though there was no subterfuge.

The Crocodile was bold in its approach. Despite swimming against the current, it was hugging close to the shore where the current was less powerful. From what Men-taur could determine, it would be positioned to attack the back of the group where he noted Vic was positioned. Concern etched Men-taur's face.

The rescuers on the bank spotted the Crocodile too. They re-doubled their encouragement and added shouts of warning. The first Beest were struggling out of the water and some rescuers hesitated, watching the progress of the Crocodile. Courage overcame fear and they resumed their duties with greater urgency and watchfulness. They knew — where there was one Crocodile there may be others.

Vic could see the approaching bank, could see some of the group had made it, but could only hear the cow against him, who was loudly snorting with effort. With added groans and fear emanating from the cow, he could not hear the shouts of warning.

Men-taur and the others on the shore could only watch as the Crocodile approached Vic and the cow from behind. The cow began to slow and her body began to sag against Vic's. His muscles ached. His joints ached. The cold water was also stealing the energy from him, yet he remained determined to get the cow ashore — he was adamant that he not going to lose another Beest. The water's edge was so close now, and he knew he had come too far to fail.

Vic eased off and angled himself so that he could push from behind the cow's shoulder. And then, two things happened at the same time: First, one of Vic's hooves found the River-bottom; second, the Crocodile reached Vic.

Vic's face reflected pain and fearful confusion. His progress had slowed. His mind said he had made it but pain raced up his back and screamed into his head. Instinct told him to drive with everything he had.

Vic turned his head to look behind him. All he glimpsed was the tip of a brown and gray leathery tail. Fear and the surge of desperate energy coursed through his body as he fully registered that he was being attacked by a Crocodile.

Vic kicked back with everything — all of his Passion, all of his Commitment, all of his Vision. Expecting to find water, Vic's feet found the snout of the Crocodile and, in that brief instant, a lancing shot of pain tore into Vic's brain and the Crocodile lost its grip.

Vic was fighting for his life, and so his flight mechanism was in overdrive, and that small gap of time before the Crocodile could relaunch its attack was all Vic needed. His adrenaline-pumped momentum carried him clear out of the water.

The immediate area along the River's edge had been cleared to a safe distance in order to protect against the Crocodile claiming a further victim. Men-taur and another rescuer came to assist Vic. The cow he had been escorting was being helped by another Beest.

"Are you alright, Vic?" Men-taur asked with deep concern as he drew alongside Vic.

Vic could only breathe and feel the pounding of his heart as it threatened to leap out of his chest. As the effects of the adrenaline rush began to abate, Vic's muscles and legs began to tremble. He stumbled.

Both Men-taur and the rescuer managed to prop him up with their bodies pressed against his on either side. "Let's get you away from here," directed Men-taur, as he began to guide Vic up the slope of the bank.

Dusk crept on. Vic could not remember reaching the top of the bank. All he remembered was Men-taur's encouraging presence. Slowly, it dawned on him that he had made it. He had survived a Crocodile attack and he had fulfilled his assignment; with that realization, relief began to wash over him. The relief brought with it a calm, which replenished Vic's ebbing energy.

Turning towards Men-taur, Vic finally answered his question. "Thank you, Men-taur. I'm alright."

As Vic turned, he winced with pain. He looked and tried to locate its origin. He could see fresh blood dripping down his left hind leg. Its source seemed to be a couple of deep puncture wounds where the Crocodile must have bitten into his flesh. The area felt very tender, but there was still some pain that he still could not account for.

Just then Men-taur replied with a chuckle, "Indeed you are, Vic. You will be fine. After all, you managed to get away from that Crocodile — but he got away with your tail."

Awareness dawned on Vic's face. He had no tail. But, to Vic, that was a small price to pay for his life. And so, despite his pain, he began to chuckle too.

Men-taur smiled and added with a hint of mirth, "Ahh, so you can see the lighter side of your injury. Good. A very healthy attitude. Now, I'll give you some time to recover and lick your wounds — literally. I must now go and see that preparations have been made for the evening. It is now time for you to get some well-deserved rest. I'll speak with you in the morning." As Men-taur turned to leave, as was his habit, he added a parting encouragement, "Vic, you did exceptionally well today. You have played a significant role in the success of this Crossing. On behalf of the Herd, I thank you."

And, before Vic could reply, Men-taur was gone.

Vic was left to his own thoughts. There were only two things he could actually think of, and they were food and sleep. His stomachs were churning on empty. He had no cud left to chew. He decided - food first, and then rest.

Vic set out, albeit stiffly, in search of his desires.

Dusk blurred into evening, which blurred into night. The sky overhead was clear and glittered with a myriad of stars. The moon beamed down with its smiling face. The air was now filled with the counter-point harmony of chirruping insects and snoring Beest.

Now that he had grazed, Vic could settle down for a well-deserved sleep. Now that he felt relaxed and replenished, the full weight of the day rolled over him. Apart from an overwhelming sense of accomplishment, Vic could not figure out, try as he may, what the lesson was that Men-taur intimated was so obvious. Vic decided that, rather than get frustrated, which would subsequently prevent him from sleeping, he would get fascinated with the lesson as it unfolded in the morning. Until then, it was time to sleep.

Vic surrendered to his fatigue. His was a deep and restful sleep.

...rather than get frustrated... get fascinated.

The annoying buzz of flies awoke Vic. Vic winced. His stump of a tail had automatically attempted to swat away the flies. As his tail or lack thereof would not be effective, he shook his head and got quickly to his feet. His body seemed to ache all over. He stretched and took in some long, slow draughts of air to help clear his head.

Once the fog had cleared from his thoughts, Vic set out purposefully in search of Men-taur. He had an inkling now as to what the lesson was about and excitement buzzed as he wanted to confirm it.

Rather than wade through the milling center of the Herd, Vic skirted along the Edge. He reasoned that Men-taur would be somewhere close to the most forward point of the Herd. As he progressed, he received several acknowledgements from various Beest, and one or two even thanked him for his efforts. Vic returned the greetings, although admittedly not knowing many of those who greeted him.

Soon enough, Vic found Men-taur sat atop another characteristic knoll looking out toward the Horizon. A couple of other Beest were with him. From where he was positioned, Men-taur noticed Vic's approach and dismissed the other Beest. "Good morning, Vic," greeted Men-taur warmly.

"Good morning, Men-taur." Vic drew up next to Men-taur.

"You look rested," commented Men-taur and then questioned, "How's the tail?"

In reply, Vic agreed, "Yes, I feel rested and my tail, or what's left of it, still feels sore but I'll be fine."

"Of course you'll be fine. I expect nothing less." And without further preamble, Men-taur declared, "Right. Let's review your lesson."

After the briefest of pauses, Men-taur continued, "So, Vic, tell me: Have you figured out what lesson you were to glean from this Crossing?"

"Yes, I think so. Last night I could not figure it out. I suppose I was more than likely too tired. However, I awoke this morning with a prevailing thought as to what the lesson was about. I tested it against the other lessons and realized that they had a logical flow, and so I

asked myself what would naturally flow from a decision. The answer
—taking Action."

Men-taur beamed a smile of acknowledgement. "Well done again,
Vic. Taking action is exactly right. So, let's explore what you have
learned about taking Action. Go ahead."

Lesson 6 - Action

"Well, to recap, my assignment was to first oversee the briefing of
the new Crossing procedures with an added emphasis to be voiced
concerning the buddy system. After I had crossed to this side, the
second part of my task was to coordinate the rescue teams, whereby
our role was to help those struggling to cross or those stranded at the
starting point. The entire day was a series of decision-based Action;
realizing that the group was too big to hear the briefing, I had to use
some initiative, and so Dow-taur and I agreed to break up the small
group and then delegate the briefing and the assigning of buddies to
other responsible Beest. Dow-taur, I felt, was not impressed by me,
and so I made a point of speaking to the group with deference to him,
which ultimately seemed to help us to work together—"

"Sorry to cut you off, Vic," Men-taur interrupted, "but I just wanted to
add a brief comment about initiative. If a decision is the father of Action,
then initiative is its mother; the two combine to give birth to Action."

> *If a decision is the father of Action,*
> *then initiative is its mother.*

Vic absorbed the insight and, after a moment he continued,
"I learned from my buddy, Elle-taur, that in my role I had to take control
of the group or the Crossing would control me; without Action I would
lose credibility, and so I knew I had to lead by example."

"Exactly. Exactly. Leadership is about acting on what you talk
about. After all, Beest do what Beest see," Men-taur contributed,
"Please continue."

Vic traced his thoughts and then continued.

"During the crossing I realized that Elle-taur was weakening. Despite the original idea of being upstream to my buddy, when she became troubled I was less able to help in that position, and so I opted to quickly change my plan midstream so that I was downstream to her. I swam to support her from there as it was easier to add my efforts to support hers. I was determined that she was going to make it across and I was prepared to do whatever I could to help her. This proved successful."

"So what did that teach you?" asked Men-taur.

Vic took a moment to consider his reply, then answered, "There are critical times when I must be Decisive in the moment for which I cannot always be prepared. I must rely on my knowledge and experience, make a decision and act on it proactively, quickly and confidently.
The best way I can describe it is to be prepared, and then act and readjust accordingly."

...be prepared, and then act and readjust accordingly.

Men-taur nodded.

"Once I had crossed, I teamed up with the other rescuers.
We allocated roles and designated areas of responsibility, realizing that we should position our support on both the upstream and downstream sides of the Crossing based on what we had learned. We then worked together as a team with a constant supply of replacements at each subsequent crossing. We served as visible, audible and practical encouragement and help. Our success was down, at least in part, to working as a team."

Vic paused to recall what happened next. Men-taur filled the gap.

"Action and teamwork go hand in hand, Vic. While not something I wish you to experience first hand, consider a Cheetah which has to feed her cubs. A Cheetah only has limited staying power when it is chasing prey. They are sprint specialists — the epitome of Action, I believe.
A mother Cheetah will teach her cubs to hunt using them as her team, each of them adopting their own role to play in the hunt. In a relay, they will take it in turns to run down their prey and so, as a team they

are successful; as a team they will more likely survive, whereas on their own they most likely will not."

Vic pictured what Men-taur was describing. It helped him to clarify the significance of a team and the role it plays in taking Action based on clear decisions.

Vic then continued his summary. "When we lost the two Beest to the Crocodiles, I was hurt and shocked, I suppose. My pride took it personally. And then, when Dow-taur seemingly dismissed the loss and considered the Crossing over, disregarding those stranded back on the other side, I became incensed." Vic's face clouded over with the recollection. "I just acted. I assumed control of my fear of the Crocodiles, rounded up a dedicated team of rescuers and headed back across. Once on the other side we rallied and rounded up the stragglers. It was then that we discovered we did not have enough rescuers to buddy every Beest and so, as a team, we revised the plan.

"Where we could, we paired up the strongest Beest stranded with each other and paired ourselves up with the weaker. We then stationed ourselves along the two sides of the group. In addition to the obstacle of the water and the threat it posed regarding both drowning and the Crocodiles, there was also the consideration of the nearby Lion which had spooked a couple of the group before we crossed. At this point, time was pressing and light was beginning to fail, and so we let those Beest escape without giving chase. I realized at that point that I was unable to save them all, and that sometimes it is the Way of Things whereby sacrifice of the few is required for the sake of the many."

"A valuable lesson in itself," Men-taur added sadly.

Vic concluded, "The fear of the Lion helped us to create the momentum we needed to get the group into the River. Our phalanx idea worked well. We got all the Beest across although, I must admit, the Crocodile did surprise me."

Men-taur looked over at Vic and then started to laugh. Vic joined in. There was nothing quite like a near-death experience to put life into perspective.

Once the mirth had subsided, Men-taur congratulated Vic. "I am not sure, Vic, how aware you are of just how successful that Crossing was. We have never had a safer Crossing. We lost only a tenth of what we lost on the last Crossing. Most of our result is attributed to both your ideas and the Action of both yourself and your team. I cannot thank you enough; the Herd and I are indebted to you. Thank you for making this the safest Journey of my Vision."

As he finished, Men-taur bowed in honor and respect for Vic. Vic shifted uneasily under the praise with his eyes averting Men-taur's. He smiled uncomfortably, accepting the respect and gratitude humbly.

Men-taur then filled the ensuing silence as Vic, clearly, was not about to say anything. "Time for me to summarize the lesson. Our lives here on the plains are about survival. Only the fittest survive. The fittest are usually also the best at taking Action on their decisions. This is true at an individual level as well as at a team or Herd level. To survive and to achieve any outcome requires Action.

...to achieve any outcome requires Action.

"Vic, you have proven yourself to be both giving and selfless in your commitment to the assignment. You have inspired me and I am sure you have inspired others, which Is no mean feat for someone so young, let me assure you. Now as you may be aware," Men-taur concluded, "once we crossed the River this second time, it marked the completion of another Journey. With its completion comes your final lesson Vic. But, you will have to wait for a few more days once we have moved away from the River and deeper into the plains where the grass is green, rich and plentiful at this time. I know, Vic, that you will enjoy this last lesson. And so, until next time, you will have to excuse me — I have some duties to attend to. Enjoy this time."

Men-taur did not move, and Vic instinctively knew that this was his cue to excuse himself.

"Thank you, Men-taur," Vic said in parting.

"You're welcome," Men-taur replied as he watched quietly and proudly as Vic headed down the knoll and off into the Herd.

Vic resumed his day with a big smile.

"Success...seems to be connected with action.
Successful men keep moving.
They make mistakes, but they don't quit."

Conrad Hilton

"There are risks and costs to a program of action.
But they are far less than the long-range risks
and costs of comfortable in action."

JFK

Exercise 6 - Your Taking Action

As with the previous exercises, please consider this exercise carefully and thoughtfully, as it pertains to successfully achieving your Vision that you noted previously.

1. On a scale of 1-10*, how quick and effective are you at taking Action on your decisions to achieve your Vision you wrote down for Exercise 1? _____

2. In the event that you scored yourself below an 8, what 3 things do you need to be and/or do which will increase your effectiveness of taking Action on your decisions to achieve your Vision to an 8+?

_____

_____

_____

_____

_____

_____

_____

_____

_____

_____

_____

_____

_____

_____

_____

* For this and the other exercises, please note that a score of 1 represents the weakest and a score of 10 represents the strongest.

Chapter Ten

*"Your happiest moments are along the way,
not at the end of the trip.
Rejoice this day."*

Unknown

"It's kind of fun to do the impossible."

Walt Disney

Life was in full swing on the plains. The sun was ever-present, giving forth its energy which brought Life in so many ways. The wind caressed and massaged the land as if working out its aches and pains. The rain fell in short refreshing bursts of its elixir from which Nature thirstily drank.

The marvel of Life that teamed across the grasslands — whether it was in the sky above, on the Earth below or under the Earth — all continued on its inexorable Circle of Life, linked uniquely and interdependently.

Vic hardly noticed. He spent his time over the several days since the Crossing in a reverent and contemplative mood. His body moved on automatic, and his mind and heart seemed to be working as one, integrating his last lesson on taking Action with the other five core lessons which he had been blessed to have received from Men-taur.

The dull throb of where Vic's tail had once been had begun to subside. In comparison, the memory of his encounter with the Crocodile was growing in clarity and significance; only now, upon looking back, did he begin to realize just how close he had come to his own demise.

Vic's first Journey was nearing completion. The simple fact of that truth was only just beginning to register. And, while he knew he was not the first nor would he be the last Beest to endure the Journey, the impact of it, he knew, would be with him for his entire Life.

The Herd had now taken its final turn in the Journey which would lead them back to the widened grasslands where all the Herds would come together to recover, rejuvenate and repopulate. After that, the Cycle would start again.

Today, Vic awoke to a sense that something had changed. He could not, however, determine whether it was from within him or around him or even beyond. All he knew was that there seemed to be a different tone to the conversations buzzing around him; a tone that suggested expectation. Vic partially attributed that to the forthcoming calving season, but he also felt there was more.

Despite all that Vic had both done and achieved, whenever he attempted to engage any adult in conversation — especially when he questioned them about the buzz in the air — he was greeted with a wry and knowing smile and, subsequently, quickly dismissed with an encouraging, "You'll understand soon".

After what seemed countless efforts to extract some useful information through the morning, Vic finally chose to not expend any more energy on trying to establish the cause of the excitement. After all, he had now been informed by enough adults across the width and length of the Herd that he would soon understand and, with his contemplative mood, that was okay by him. As such, he let go of his quest and headed towards the leading Edge. There, beyond the Herd, was now a place of revelation for him, a place where he could see the Horizon more clearly which would ultimately lead to his Vision.

Because he was intent on viewing the Horizon, Vic sought out a suitable vantage point. The Herd had begun to slow down early today and he was curious as to why — a question which Vic intended to pose to Men-taur when next he saw him.

Soon, the density of Beest thinned out, indicating that Vic had arrived at the Edge. Looking outwards, Vic could partly see why the Herd was slowing; there was another Herd of Beest approaching on an intersect course. The Herd would want to ensure that proper courtesies were seen to, and that boundaries were clearly set and respected by both groups. As it happened, Vic noticed a couple of sentries heading out to meet with the other Herd.

Vic was curious. As his attention was engrossed in what was unfolding before him, Vic did not hear Men-taur approach. "Ehhemmm!" interrupted Men-taur.

All four of Vic's feet left the ground briefly as he whipped his head around in Men-taur's direction. "Oh! Sorry, Men-taur, you startled me," Vic uttered as he landed.

"Good day, Vic!" chuckled Men-taur. "Glad to see you up front here." Then with a cryptic grin, Men-taur added, "it's where the Action is and will be."

Vic simply grinned back, "I had just come up here to get some answers."

"Mind if I ask first what the questions are? Only then am I best able to help you answer them," chipped in Men-taur.

"Well, Men-taur, I really only have two questions," began Vic's reply, "One has been partially answered. That question pertained to the reason as to why the Herd was slowing down early. I think I know the answer to that one — the converging Herd. The second question is about finding out why there is a buzz in the Herd. Again, I think that the answer may well be the same. I suppose the converging of Herds brings with it an excitement and opportunity to share the excitement of another completed Journey."

"You got the first question right and the second one partially correct," agreed Men-taur with a knowing smile, "but the answer to the second one will be answered fully later today as the sun lengthens the shadows."

"I am getting used to hearing that answer today," smiled Vic. "My next lesson wouldn't by any chance be about patience?" prodded Vic.

"No, it is not, Vic," Men-taur quickly replied with a smile. After a brief pause though, Men-taur then added, again with that smile, "Now, as you have brought up the topic of your next lesson, there is no time like the present. After all, I did promise your next lesson would occur shortly after the Crossing."

Vic smiled then replied cheekily, "So I assume that means that you will be wanting me to summarize the last lesson?"

Both of them sensed the lightness in their conversation because each widened their smiles. The smiles got wider and then they both broke into spontaneous laughter. Vic could only attribute this to the fact that the Journey was now at completion and laughter was a great way to celebrate an inward feeling of joy.

Eventually, the spasms of laughter dwindled to a point where Men-taur could at least answer the questions. Beest around them had just looked in their direction briefly and contributed their own smile and buoyant spirits to the atmosphere.

"Yes, yes, Vic. That would be a good place to start," quipped Men-taur. "Once you have summarized, we can then continue on to your final lesson."

With the previous lesson still fresh in his mind — and the physical scars to remind himself — the recall proved easy. "The last lesson was concerned with taking Action and was centered around the responsibilities and associated accountabilities you set for me with the Crossing. A key part of the learning resulted from having to work alongside Dow-taur — a leader — to brief, prepare and successfully bring across a whole group from the Herd. Once on the other side of the River, my additional learning came from working with a team of rescuers with the aim of enhancing the safety of the Herd as it crossed over in successive groups."

"Throughout the day I learned that all and each of my Actions were the direct result of the choices I had to make — choices that I made in advance or that I had to make in the moment. The Actions based on advanced decisions were proactive and were accompanied by necessary preparation and planning. At times, I was required to be Decisive and make critical, spur-of-the-moment decisions, realizing that some of my decisions would have consequences. These were often determined by unexpected factors and required the ability to adapt, to be flexible and to show initiative in the execution of the plan. In one instance a decision I made I know led to the sacrifice of a few Beest, but that sacrifice of those few Beest was outweighed by the benefit to the Herd as a greater whole. From my understanding, it is important to be prepared; Action must be adaptable. That adaptability, where required, then allows for the most effective result to be achieved."

"Now, when looking back," reflected Vic, "I believe I adopted a leadership role which I did not appreciate at the time."

At this point, Men-taur smiled knowingly and nodded encouragingly.

Vic smiled back and continued. "The Crossing is a good example of leading by example. As you said, Beest do what Beest see. Your Vision, Men-taur, is about ensuring the safest Journey each time you lead the Herd. Your Vision is about ensuring the fitness of the Herd. And success of our Journey is dependent on your leadership. Your leadership is dependent on the decisions you make for the Herd and on the Actions you take to bring about your Vision. In short, success requires Action."

Vic concluded and looked over at Men-taur who was chewing his cud pensively.

Success requires Action.

Men-taur swallowed quickly, "As always, Vic, a very good summary. By linking taking Action with leadership and my Vision, you have shown that you have integrated and assimilated the lesson well, as you have with the others. With each successive lesson you have shown the ability to both absorb the current lesson and to also slot it in with the previous ones. I am absolutely convinced that these lessons will serve you well and you will honor me and the Herd in their application on a daily basis." Men-taur smiled and considered his thoughts for a moment before continuing. "If I may add a useful insight to yours, Vic, about leadership: Your leadership is only valid when others follow. The best leaders in the Herd are those who are committed to serving those they lead; the worst leaders are those who are committed only to serving themselves.

Your leadership is only valid when others follow.
The best leaders...are those who are committed
to serving those they lead; the worst leaders
are those who are committed only
to serving themselves.

After allowing Vic a few moments to absorb his view, Men-taur changed topics with a boost of enthusiasm. "Now, on to your seventh and final lesson. Casting your mind back to your first lesson, we discussed your ability to sense the Rhythm. Do you remember that?"

"Yes, Men-taur," Vic replied then recalled, "You said that only a select few animals within the Journey are highly attuned to the Rhythm and that such animals usually rise to leadership because they ensure that Balance is maintained, the Circle of Life plays out and that the Journey continues."

"Very good, Vic. So, tell me, what have you noticed about your ability to sense the Rhythm as the lessons have continued?"

"Well... with each successive lesson I feel more keenly aware of what is going on around me, within others and within myself. I suppose my understanding of things has grown with each lesson. I have learned and experienced that each lesson interlocks with the others; it is as if the lessons are seated deep within me and are creating a foundation of strength from which to live Life to the full."

"Perfect, Vic!" Men-taur exclaimed. "Living life to the full is a natural outcome when you live in tune with the Rhythm; living life to the full is a key part of the final lesson and will help you to make your final distinctions and truly be a student of the Rhythm."

As often was the case, when Men-taur wanted to make an impact he paused. Vic waited expectantly.

Eventually, Men-taur added, "This final lesson can only truly be experienced. You cannot learn it by talking about it or believing it to be true. In actual fact, every Beest should experience the final lesson, even if they do not experience or understand fully, or in part, the others. Today, the Herd as a whole will experience this lesson — not just you" Men-taur declared.

It was only then that Vic realized that the Herd had been slowly coming up behind and around them, and were concentrating along an undetected line just ahead of them. All heads were facing in the direction of the converging Herd. From what Vic could determine, based on the general direction and speed of the movement of both

Herds, they would meet around a large, lone acacia tree beneath which lay a large slab of gray, weatherworn rock.

Men-taur then pressed towards the leading Edge. Beest gave way with respectful and knowing nods. Then Men-taur stopped and looked over at Vic who habitually had fallen into step beside Men-taur. "So, rather than give it away, as with your two most recent lessons, I will let you figure it out for yourself. You stay here with the Herd. As you can see, we are about to meet with the other Herd now so I must go and meet their leader. We will catch up later today to summarize your lesson. Just keep your eyes and ears open."

Vic obediently stayed put as Men-taur began to move away. He was slightly unsettled because he hadn't even been given an assignment or told, even remotely, what this final lesson was all about.

As had happened with some of his previous lessons, Men-taur appeared to read Vic's mind for he turned his head, smiled and stated, "The lesson will be all around you."

The pressing crowd then engulfed Men-taur.

Vic felt adrift and unsure as to what to do. Rather than allow his confusion to pervade, he decided to just stop and breathe deeply. After three slow and deep breaths, Vic's head had cleared and he decided to follow in Men-taur's wake. He actually unexpectedly made good progress as some Beest gave way with a nod and those knowing smiles that had bothered him earlier.

Soon, Vic broke through the ranks. Out there, beneath the acacia tree, Men-taur was meeting who Vic presumed to be the leader of the other Herd. A Beest flanked each leader on either side.

From this distance, Vic could at least see that the other leader was a powerful Beest who was even larger than Men-taur, although he could not tell the age of the other leader. Vic wished he could be out at that meeting to hear what was being said. As was his want, Vic was curious to know what was going on.

A gentle wind was stirring the tops of the verdant carpet of lush grass that filled the expanse between the two Herds. Occasionally, as Vic watched, a booming laugh floated on the wind. It appeared to emanate from the other leader with whom Men-taur was meeting. It was an infectious laugh for the Beest around Vic began to chuckle. However, Vic only smiled; he did not laugh as he felt almost isolated, and that he was missing something.

The sun moved across the azure blue sky. Its heat deepened the haze that hung near the ground. The eagles circled effortlessly on the rising thermals. Termite mounds stood as sentinels across the plain. The wind ebbed. Time stood still. Nature appeared to be holding its breath.

Vic remained transfixed on the blurring image of the two leaders, while straining to make out any hint of what was being said.

Suddenly, nearby, Vic noted that a colony of Meerkat had emerged from their burrows. They appeared oblivious to events going on around them other than two animals that stood erect and vigilant atop their own dead and dry branch, likely left abandoned by some elephant some time ago. A couple of others seemed to have decided it was time to play, and they continued with what appeared to be a game of tag — chase-and-tackle — that was played with great energy and zeal. The game appeared to have no real rules and, from what Vic could tell, the Meerkat seemed to relish just having fun. There was no animosity or aggression; there was what Vic could only be described as playful banter.

As the Meerkat's game progressed, more and more of the colony joined in. Gradually, it was just one big melee that was punctuated by various squeaks and barks of varying intensity. Occasionally, a Meerkat managed to extricate itself from the playful throng and was replaced by one of the sentries. With an encouraging bark from the new sentry, the other would jump down from its vantage point and join in the fun. No Meerkat appeared to be excluded.

Vic couldn't help but smile and chuckle as he watched the fun. He could not recall the last time when he had such fun. It had been so long — too long. "Perhaps I have taken things a bit too seriously..." Vic mused.

As the haze prevented him from seeing much of the meeting out on the plain, Vic continued to watch the Meerkat, occasionally lowering his head to grab a few mouthfuls of the succulent, untrampled grass. At one point, the game steered in Vic's direction. The other Beest around him seemed to back away as a couple of Meerkat tumbled out of the frenzy. Oblivious to Vic's presence, they bumped into his lowered muzzle and then turned, barely startled, only to gently scold Vic for being in their way. They then each directed a small squeak in his direction before looking at each other, barking and diving back into their game. Vic felt like they had made a joke, delivered a punchline and only they got it.

A dawning realization then came over Vic. Within him, something seemed to suddenly melt away, and Vic began to laugh. Really laugh. It was a cleansing laugh; a spontaneous laugh; a laugh which emanated from his core, and one that seemed to instantly wash away the stress and strain of the Journey; a laugh that re-energized and restored; a laugh that brought with it a new perspective on Life.

Beest started to look in his direction. Vic did not really care what they were thinking, but instead opted to just enjoy the moment.

Eventually, the Meerkat seemed to realize they should get on with their day. The play slowed but the chatter still excitedly continued. Some disappeared into their burrows while others started to head off at a sprightly pace in search of their next meal.

Vic was still chuckling as he turned his attention to where Men-taur was, or rather, where he had been. Men-taur and the other leader seemed to have gone their own separate ways while Vic had been entranced by the Meerkat's excitement.

As Vic began to wonder if he should seek out Men-taur, the Herd began to move as one towards the slab of rock. As they did so, the other Herd also began to move to close the distance. With the movement, the adult Beest around him stopped their conversations and began to bawl in melodic unison. Vic began to move also. He soon caught the bawling's rhythmic pattern and joined in with looks of approval from those nearby.

Though Vic did not understand what was going on, he nevertheless sensed that this would be something of great significance. Mindful of

Men-taur's advice, he focused his attention and all of his senses. He could sense the building excitement and expectation; he could sense the ground seeming to reverberate with the marching hooves and the rumbling harmony of the multitude.

The advancing fronts of both Herds now stopped a short distance away from the slab of rock and the gnarled and weathered tree. The expanse of each Herd fanned out in opposite directions until the tree and rock became the focal point, completely encircled by Beest; the only indication of where one began and the other stopped was that there was a bisecting corridor of grass which seemingly created two semi-circles. The rock and tree sat as an island in the middle of the Herds.

The sun's beams seemed to focus on the rock as the tree cast a shadow to its base. From opposite ends of the corridor emerged Men-taur and the other leader. Together, they proceeded and climbed the rock slab into the focused sunlight.

Both lowered their horns. The bawling stopped.

Vic was fortunate that he was towards the front and was almost directly before where Men-taur and the other leader stood. Along with all the other Beest, he looked up. He could now see that the other bull was younger than Men-taur.

"GREETINGS!" boomed Men-taur.

A hushed silence followed.

"Once again, we come together to celebrate the completion of another Journey," continued Men-taur loudly with his voice carrying easily on the air, "For some, it was your first, for the rest of us, it was our next."

Some light laughter rippled through the combined Herds.

"On behalf of Laf-taur and myself," Men-taur projected, acknowledging his fellow leader with a respectful nod, "we would like to congratulate you for your successful arrival. Yes, there have been some who have not made it on this Journey, and let us look on their departure as a testimony to their commitment and as a worthy sacrifice for all of us who stand here today. Let us consider that they still abide with us in our hearts and in our memories. They have helped us to continue on with the Circle of Life. We honor them now with our thanks and praise."

With that last accolade, Men-taur stopped. As he did, Laf-taur let out a deep and long bellow which hung in the air like a banner over the combined Herds. As it began to dwindle, the Herd answered with a bellow that reverberated from every direction. The ground shook; the acacia tree trembled. The power of the praise ascended to the heavens. Vic's body shook and his mane rippled. As he added his bellow of tribute to that of the massed Herd, within himself he sensed the bellow emanating from the Rhythm; the sheer power and wonder of it made him feel more alive than he ever had before.

Laf-taur bowed his head. Instantly, the bellowing stopped as each head also bowed, this time in silent tribute to the lost and the fallen of this Journey.

Laf-taur then raised his head and spoke with no further hint of solemnity. "Each and every one of us has achieved this milestone, having passed a few more along the way. The Journey is never-ending. And so, each milestone along the way must be celebrated; without celebrating our achievements, our lives lack purpose and meaning.

...without celebrating our achievements our lives lack purpose and meaning.

"You may not have had a chance to celebrate as yet; after all, the Journey has just reached completion and is hard work. No doubt you all required rest and recuperation. Now, however, today is a chance for you to reward yourselves and to reward each other with congratulations and praise. You kept moving forward. You lived by the golden rule- *'Hoof it!'*. You made it!" Laf-taur then reared, shook his horns and let out a triumphant bellow. The Herd joined in. Vic joined the Herd. Half a million Beest all rearing and bellowing was both a sight and sound to behold; no predator would have dared to come close, such was the power of the moment.

As Laf-taur lowered himself, so did the Herd. Silence once again descended on the gathering.

Men-taur then stepped forward and lifted his head high. "As those who have gone before, you will realize that the completion of one's first Journey is a significant milestone which comes with its own special reward. For those of you near-yearlings, this is a rite of passage.

"Laf-taur and I appreciate that this honor must be bestowed on each of you. As it is the Way of Things, we have selected a representative from the near-yearlings to join us now."

The Herd waited. Vic was wondering what all of this meant when two elders approached him and beckoned him forward. Vic looked around wondering who they were looking at, as there were a few other near-yearlings nearby. Vic looked back towards the elders and the intensity of their gaze said it all. Realizing it was his presence they were requesting, he stepped forward and the two elders immediately flanked him as they steered him up onto the slab.

As Vic ascended to join Laf-taur and Men-taur, he began to see the full expanse of the spectacle of the gathered Herds. He was in awe and suddenly felt daunted. Added to that, Vic had no idea as to what was about to happen and, at that very moment, he would rather have faced a Crocodile.

As he approached, Laf-taur greeted him with the warmest and most welcoming of smiles. When he looked at Men-taur, Vic saw a mirrored smile. Together, their smiles melted away the anxiety which had begun to well up inside of him. The two leaders turned as one with Vic in the center. Despite the encouraging and relaxed smiles, Vic felt overwhelmed by what was going on.

Finally, Men-taur spoke out. "In honor of all you near-yearlings and your key role in the continuation of the Journey and the Circle of Life, I bring before you and to the rest of the Herd, your representative, Vic. Today, all of you now have earned the full privileges as a member of the Herd. With that, you are, from this day forward, to be known by your new and full name. All of you are now entitled to complete your name. And so I honor before you — VIC-TAUR!" Men-taur bellowed.

Men-taur let that declaration ring out across the Herds, and then the entire Herd began chanting Vic-taur's new name.

Vic, or rather Vic-taur, did not know what to do or where to look. Men-taur leaned over and whispered in his ear, "You deserve this". Vic was stunned; he had never been curious about the difference in names between calves and adults, nor had he ever even made the connection regarding the '–taur' ending. How could he not have noticed?

Just as Vic was feeling overwhelmed by all the attention, Laf-taur once again signaled for all to be quiet. "Now that the formal part of this gathering is nearing completion, all that is left to say is — let the celebrations begin! You all have earned it! Enjoy yourselves! Today is a time for all of us to have some fun, so laugh, play and have fun! Before you know it, we will once again have to 'Hoof it!'"

And with that, Laf-taur began to laugh a deep, rich laugh which seemed to originate from the Earth itself. In response, the Herd let out a vibrant cheer, mixed with infectious laughter.

The celebrations had begun.

As the Herd began to disperse, Men-taur beckoned towards Vic-taur. In a daze, Vic-taur took the few intervening steps. Men-taur then turned to Laf-taur, "Laf-taur, may I personally introduce you to Vic-taur."

Laf-taur, whose laughter had simmered to a chuckle, now greeted Vic-taur warmly. "Congratulations Vic-taur. Men-taur here tells me that you are an excellent student. He told me how you have contributed to the well-being of the Herd, and even tells me that one day you will give me some competition!" Laf-taur seemed to find humor in everything as he began to laugh again.

Vic-taur, still feeling uncomfortable with praise, replied simply and respectfully, "Thank you, Laf-taur. I have a great teacher."

Laf-taur managed to nod in agreement whilst honoring Men-taur. "Vic-taur, let me tell you, you will not find a better leader than Men-taur; he has taught me all I know about leadership and being a success."

Vic-taur's eyes widened with surprise.

"Yes, that's right, Vic-taur, I was like you just a few Journeys ago. I am where I am today because of Men-taur."

Now it was Men-taur's turn to become uncomfortable. The only outward sign was a slight uneasy shifting of his hooves.

"Vic-taur, do you mind me asking you something?" Without waiting for a response, Laf-taur continued, "I am guessing that today is to be your final lesson, right?"

"Uhh... yes, how did you know?" Vic-taur asked.

Laf-taur first winked at Men-taur, who now looked bemused, and then revealed, "The same thing happened to me. Men-taur is predictable... sometimes!" Already beginning to laugh, Laf-taur added, "As it is your last lesson, I will not interrupt you further because I know that you are just about to tell Men-taur what you have learned today, right, Men-taur?"

"Off with you Laf-taur. You are incorrigible!" exclaimed Men-taur, adding his own laugh to the mix.

Not wanting to be left out and feeling the lightness of the mood, Vic-taur joined in too.

Still laughing, Laf-taur excused himself and left to join the celebration.

"Okay, Vic-taur," began Men-taur, "Laf-taur has stolen my thunder just a little. As the Herd around us is celebrating, we appear to have been given an island of calm to explore what you have learned about this, your seventh and final lesson. Once we are finished, we can join in the fun and games. So, Vic-taur, what can you tell me about today's lesson? What do you think it is about?"

Vic-taur answered, "Well, as you mentioned earlier, Men-taur, when I paid attention, the lesson would be everywhere today. What I have noticed everywhere today is the importance of having fun and celebrating success."

"Exactly," agreed Men-taur. "Your lesson is about Fun. So, considering I told you to pay attention today, tell me what you learned. Let's see how much you picked up, huh?" Men-taur was in a good mood. Vic-taur would even have described it as playful. Keeping that in mind, Vic-taur realized that even a leader must know how to have Fun and show it.

Lesson 7 - Fun

And so Vic-taur started there. "Men-taur, from what I have seen today of you and Laf-taur, I now realize how important it is for a leader to know how to have Fun. As we discussed during the last lesson, 'Beest do what Beest see'. How can the Herd expect to enjoy themselves and have Fun if the leaders don't show them how?"

*...even a leader must know how to
have Fun and show it.*

Men-taur validated Vic-taur's observation. "Vic-taur, that is a key point with respect to this lesson as well as the others. Laf-taur, as if you could not tell, really took on board this last lesson; regardless of what we are facing, it is important to be able to see the lighter side. To give you an example, Vic-taur, do you remember when you lost your tail to that Crocodile and we managed to muster a laugh about it?"

"Yes", Vic-taur replied with a slight smile.

"I noted that you could have easily begun to bemoan the loss of your tail. By doing so, you would have ultimately stolen some joy and sense of achievement from your Crossing and from surviving such an attack. You are young but you may already have heard the expression, 'In the future, you will look back at this and laugh'?"

Vic-taur nodded.

"That expression is usually spoken when some hardship or difficult challenge has arisen which has consequently dampened a Beest's spirits. Well, why wait until later, I always say! Laugh now!"

*Why wait until later...
Laugh now!*

"Enjoyment can be found in everything, Vic-taur; sometimes, you just have to look harder. Throughout the Journeys, there will always be challenges, and so always ensure that they are kept in the perspective that you are alive." Men-taur finished with an upbeat tone as if to highlight the significance of the wisdom.

Enjoyment can be found in everything;
sometimes you just have to look harder.

Vic-taur reflected for a moment and then spoke. "I realize that I would do well to be less serious and look upon everything as a blessing. From that perspective, it would be easier for me in the future to enjoy each moment and challenge. Our day-to-day lives can be perceived as either dull, dreary work or just plain fun. Fun is a matter of choice."

Fun is a matter of choice.

This time, Men-taur simply nodded. Vic-taur reviewed the day in his mind quickly and then continued on with his observations and learnings. "From the time I awoke today, I noticed that there was a building excitement and expectation amongst those who have Journeyed before; for those of us for whom this was our first, we got caught-up in the momentum of it without having the full realization of what it was about. I watched a family of Meerkat take time to just play and have Fun; it started seemingly spontaneously with just two, and then it spread through the family like an excitable fire.

Even considering the need to be watchful, their sentries were relieved of their responsibility so they could also join in the Fun. Once they had had enough Fun they returned to the more routine tasks of the day and with what I thought was a bit more energy." Vic smiled as he considered his thoughts. "Their comical escapades caused me to laugh spontaneously, for some reason. All the harshness and weariness I had felt from the Journey then just left me. I felt re-energized."

Men-taur interjected, "Again, Vic-taur, you have hit on the core aspect of this lesson. Fun can be contagious — if we allow it to be. If you had not noticed, Laf-taur's attitude and playful nature is infectious; no-one leaves a meeting with him without feeling uplifted. We can always endure more when we are lighter of spirit."

Fun can be contagious — if we allow it to be.

Vic-taur soaked up the significance of what Men-taur was saying before continuing. "The gathering of the Herds clearly had a purpose for the Herd to take dedicated time out to celebrate the completion of the Journey. This is a key milestone of achievement for any Beest, or other plains' animals, for that matter. Considering that we never know when our days will end, I understand now how important it is to celebrate each milestone, regardless of whether it is a big one, such as the Journey, or a smaller, yet no-less significant one, such as a Crossing."

We can always endure more
when we are lighter of spirit.

"When we celebrate our achievements, big or small, we are rewarding ourselves. Rewards help to energize our true purpose and to propel us on the next leg towards the Horizon and towards the ultimate achievement — our Vision. What makes a reward even more significant is the ability to share it; a reward shared is that much sweeter."

What makes a reward even more
significant is the ability to share it.

"The last insight I have relates to when I was called forward and given my full name. The honor and awe of that moment was, and still is, overwhelming. I am sure that was the same for all the others who received their full names today. What makes this even more significant though is the fact that it is linked to the mass celebration going on around us. For me, and likely the rest like me who have just become full members of the Herd, it feels like this celebration is just for me or for us. For those Beest for whom this is another Journey, the celebration likely reinforces those feelings when they took on their full name." Vic-taur ended with a slow outward breath.

At its end, Men-taur spoke up. "Vic-taur, your grasp of this lesson is exceptional as it has been with all the others. I have nothing more to add, other that it is now time for you to live up to your name. As with every name, it carries with it a blessing and purpose."

Clearing his throat, Men-taur concluded, "Vic-taur, as you now know, we have come to the end of your seven lessons. You have been an exceptional student. Though you will always be a student of the Rhythm, you have now learned the lessons which will ultimately keep you attuned to the Rhythm, so always keep those lessons fresh and the Rhythm will always be strong.

"Now, while we will see each other again, it will be as equals.
I know you will use these lessons well and you will bear them in mind,
enabling you to grow, develop and lead. I am proud of you and expect
great things from you. And, although this marks the end of the lessons,
it is not the end of your ongoing Journey. All that remains to be said is
'Hoof it!'"

Men-taur stood still. Vic-taur felt overwhelmed with gratitude.
Knowing he had just been dismissed, he bowed low in respect. As he
raised himself, he held Men-taur's gaze, sure that he could see a tear
forming, and simply exclaimed, *"Hoof it!"*

This time, it was Vic's turn to leave. And, as he did so, at the base of
the slab of rock there stood Moh. With the recognition, elation surged
through his body. Now, this Journey was complete.

Vic-taur had found his mother!

*"When we accept tough jobs as a challenge
and wade into them with joy and enthusiasm,
miracles can happen."*

Arland Gilbert

*It's the game of Life. Do I win or do I lose?
One day they're gonna shut the game down.
I gotta have as much fun and go around
the board as many times as I can before
it's my turn to leave.*

Tupac Shakur

Exercise 7 - **Your Having Fun**

As with the previous exercises, please consider this exercise carefully and thoughtfully, as it pertains to successfully achieving your Vision that you noted previously.

1. On a scale of 1-10*, what is your level of Fun you are having on your Journey to achieving your Vision that you wrote down for Exercise 1?

2. In the event that you scored yourself below an 8, what 3 things do you need to be and/or do which will increase your level of Fun you are having to an 8+?

_____

_____

_____

_____

_____

_____

_____

_____

_____

_____

_____

_____

_____

* For this and the other exercises, please note that a score of 1 represents the weakest and a score of 10 represents the strongest.

Epilogue

*"You have a calling which exists only for you
and which only you can fulfil."*

Dr. Naomi Stephan

*"We all have the extraordinary coded within us...
waiting to be released."*

Jean Houston

The sun shone down from its zenith, bathing all that lived and all that didn't. Gathered around the ancient acacia were the leaders and future leaders of all grazing and foraging Herds which had endured the Journey — Zebra, Gazelle, Impala, Wildebeest and others. Today was the first such gathering ever.

Now, another Journey was about to begin in the continuation of the Circle of Life. Today was Vic-taur's first forum of the School of Success, which he had envisioned nearly five Journeys ago; its purpose was to help one and all and their respective Herds to work together to improve the Circle of Life.

As Vic-taur stood at the base of that old slab of rock, he marveled at the path which had led him to this point. Looking over at Moh, who was smiling encouragingly, he realized that had he not been separated from her shortly after his birth, he would never have met Men-taur and, without Men-taur, he would never have learned those crucially important life lessons. Not a day went by when Vic-taur did not live each of those essential learnings: Vision, Passion, Commitment, being prepared to Change and Learn, being Decisive, Action and having Fun.

Now was the result of living them. Now he was the newly appointed leader of his Herd. Now Vic-taur was convening his first School of Success.

Vic-taur wondered what Men-taur would have thought had he been here. Though he had left the Circle on the last Journey, Vic-taur realized just how much he missed and owed his old teacher, but he nevertheless realized that death was all part of the Circle of Life — it was the Way of Things.

Vic-taur smiled, looked to the sky and quietly said, "Thank you."

He ascended the rock and began. "It is time for all of us to work together. To do that there are seven key lessons, which I wish to impart; seven principles which I, myself, learned from an old friend." And, as he spoke, Vic-taur was sure he heard Men-taur's voice on the wind declare...

"Hoof it!"

"You cannot teach a man anything.
You can only help him discover it
within himself."

Galileo Galilei

"Wow!" This is a book that, through the concepts it has brought to light, will impact thousands of people and will undoubtedly touch again and again. This book is not to be read once but, over and over as one journey's through life. I am so excited to send this to so many people I know. This book will be a profoundly positive influence in everyone's "Circle of Life."

Rob Gimbl *– former CLO Citigroup*

Find Out More

Bring *Hoof it!* Alive

For more information about Richard Norris's workshops, webinars, speaking engagements, coaching programs and other resources, please visit

www.hoofitbook.com

1241365R0

Printed in Great Britain by
Amazon.co.uk, Ltd.,
Marston Gate.